Unrivaled Christ, Unstoppable Gospel,
Unreached Peoples, Unending Joy

CROSS

JOHN PIPER AND DAVID MATHIS, GENERAL EDITORS

PUBLISHING GROUP

NASHVILLE, TENNESSEE

978-1-4336-8601-6

Published by B&H Publishing Group
Nashville, Tennessee

Dewey Decimal Classification: 266
Subject Heading: MISSIONS \ WITNESSING \
EVANGELISTIC WORK

Italics used in Scripture is author's emphasis.

1 2 3 4 5 6 7 8 • 19 18 17 16 15

CONTENTS

CONTRIBUTORS

Thabiti Anyabwile is assistant pastor for church planting at Capitol Hill Baptist Church in Washington, D.C.; he served previously as pastor of First Baptist Church of Grand Cayman. He is a native of Lexington, North Carolina, and is the author of *The Gospel for Muslims: An Encouragement to Share Christ with Confidence*. He is the happy husband of Kristie and the adoring father of three children.

Don Carson is research professor of New Testament at Trinity Evangelical Divinity School in Deerfield, Illinois. He has served as assistant pastor and pastor, has done itinerant ministry in Canada and the United Kingdom, and is cofounder (with Tim Keller) and president of The Gospel Coalition. He has written or edited over fifty books, including *How Long, O Lord? Reflections on Suffering and Evil* and *A Call to Spiritual Reformation*. He and his wife, Joy, have two grown children and live in Libertyville, Illinois.

Matt Chandler serves as lead pastor for teaching at The Village Church in Dallas, Texas, and is involved in church planting around the world through The Village Church and other partnerships such as Acts 29, which he serves as president. He is the author of *The Explicit Gospel* and *Creature of the Word*. He and his wife, Lauren, live with their three children in Highland Village, Texas.

Richard Chin serves as the National Director of the Australian Fellowship of Evangelical Students, and the South Pacific Regional

Secretary for the International Fellowship of Evangelical Students. Based at Wollongong University, he also serves as a University chaplain with a team that proclaims Christ to local and international students. He is a Malaysian-born Chinese Aussie.

Kevin DeYoung is pastor at University Reformed Church in East Lansing, Michigan. He is the author of several books, including *The Hole in Our Holiness, The Good News We Almost Forgot,* and *Just Do Something*. Kevin and his wife, Trisha, have five children.

David Mathis is executive editor at desiringGod.org, elder at Cities Church, Minneapolis, and adjunct professor for Bethlehem College & Seminary. He is coeditor of *Finish the Mission: The Cost of Bringing the Gospel to the Unreached and Unengaged* and coauthor of *How to Stay Christian in Seminary*. He and his wife, Megan, have three children.

Conrad Mbewe worked as a mining engineer in Zambia before answering God's call into pastoral ministry and has been pastor at Kabwata Baptist Church in Lusaka, Zambia, since 1987. He maintains a full itinerant preaching ministry in different countries around the world and edits *Reformation Zambia* magazine. Conrad volunteers with the YMCA, providing vocational training to the many unemployed youths in his community. He is married to Felistas and has three children and two foster daughters.

Michael Oh is the executive director of the Lausanne Movement. He is the founder of CBI Japan which includes a graduate level theological seminary (Christ Bible Seminary), church planting efforts (All NationsFellowship), and various outreach ministries (including the Heart & Soul Café). He and his wife Pearl have five children.

John Piper is founder and teacher for desiringGod.org and chancellor of Bethlehem College & Seminary, Minneapolis. For more than thirty years, he served as pastor at Bethlehem Baptist Church. He is the author of more than fifty books, including *Desiring God* and *Let the Nations Be Glad: The Supremacy of God in Missions*, and coeditor of *Finish the Mission: The Cost of Bringing the Gospel to the Unreached and Unengaged*. More than thirty years of his preaching and teaching ministry is available at desiringGod.org. John and his wife, Noël, have four sons, one daughter, and twelve grandchildren.

David Platt is the president of the International Mission Board of the Southern Baptist Convention. For eight years, he served as pastor of The Church at Brook Hills in Birmingham, Alabama. He is author of *Radical: Taking Back Your Faith from the American Dream*. He and his wife Heather are parents of three children.

Mack Stiles is CEO of Gulf Digital Solutions and general secretary for the Fellowship of Christian UAE Students (FOCUS) in the United Arab Emirates. He has worked for many years with InterVarsity Christian Fellowship in the United States. He is the author of *Marks of the Messenger* and *Speaking of Jesus*. He is married to Leeann, and they are parents of three sons.

Beautiful Feet

David Mathis

How beautiful upon the mountains are the feet of him who brings good news, who publishes peace, who brings good news of happiness.

(Isa. 52:7)

What would it sound like to receive an invitation from the most important person alive, to join him in the most important venture on the planet?

Perhaps he would reference what he's done in the past, and how it connects with this initiative—that he "became a servant" in the incarnation, not only "to show God's truthfulness" and "confirm the promises given to the patriarchs," but also "that the Gentiles might glorify God for his mercy" (Rom. 15:8–9).

Maybe he would outline the mission and pledge its fulfillment: "I have other sheep that are not of this fold. I must bring them also, and they will listen to my voice. So there will be one flock, one shepherd" (John 10:16).

1

Likely such a personage would make unblushing promises of reward, despite the drawbacks: "Truly, I say to you, there is no one who has left house or brothers or sisters or mother or father or children or lands, for my sake and for the gospel, who will not receive a hundredfold now in this time, houses and brothers and sisters and mothers and children and lands, with persecutions, and in the age to come eternal life" (Mark 10:28–30).

He may even be so bold as to say, "If anyone would come after me, let him deny himself and take up his cross and follow me. For whoever would save his life will lose it, but whoever loses his life for my sake and the gospel's will save it" (Mark 8:34–35). The venture would be so significant (and no doubt, the attendant cost is so great) that it might sound off-putting at first—until the pledge sinks in, and you realize how "inescapably hedonistic"[1] such an offer is.

Given his inherited resources and his own acquired power, he may let you know that finishing the task is not just likely, but absolutely certain. "This gospel of the kingdom will be proclaimed throughout the whole world as a testimony to all nations, and then the end will come" (Matt. 24:14).

And if the invitation were authentic, he may even divulge the extent of his authority, under which the endeavor will operate ("All authority in heaven and on earth has been given to me"), give specific instructions for the mission ("Go therefore and make disciples of all nations"), and promise not just his oversight and support, but his own presence and intimate involvement ("Behold, I am with you always, to the end of the age," [Matt. 28:18–20]).

One Commission, Two Callings

The reality, of course, is that *you are invited*—in all the above terms and many more biblical overtures bursting with missionary vision.

You are invited to be involved in the world's greatest initiative, to participate in the planet's biggest project, and to engage in history's most exciting enterprise. Already the decisive act has been accomplished when the Son of God himself gave his own life on a hill outside Jerusalem to secure the salvation of his people from all the peoples, and rose again victorious over sin, death, and hell. Now he leads the mission from the control room of the universe, at his Father's right hand, and by his Spirit, through his own people, he is extending his offer of life to every tribe, tongue, and nation.

This summons to wear the jersey and come onto the field with the globe's greatest team is singular and plural. Our star has only one team. All who answer his call wear the same blood-red, and don his unmistakable logo. But you may say he calls us to various positions on two distinct sides of the ball. Some he has sent to make disciples among peoples already "reached" in societies where churches already exist and pathways to his message are accessible. "Reached" doesn't mean everyone believes, or even that many believe. And it doesn't mean that the work isn't important, even essential, to his Commission. But it is fundamentally distinct from the calling he gives to others: to make disciples among the "unreached."

There is a fundamental difference: some of us complete the Commission among "reached peoples," and some of us do so among the "unreached," or even "unengaged."

Pursue All the Peoples

People groups are communities or societies of persons and families with a shared language and common ethnic identity. An *unreached* people, as mission strategists commonly use the term, is a group with no indigenous Christian community, or Christians so few in number (and without adequate resources) that they are unlikely to ably plant the gospel and the church among their people.[2] Meanwhile, an *unengaged* people is one in which no known church-planting effort is currently active.[3]

Missions, then, is a term for preserving a category for the church's evangelistic efforts to reach the unreached and engage the unengaged. Taking the gospel across the street and to one's own friends and family and coworkers and associates is vital. This is the work of local mission, which we often call *evangelism*—or if that word carries too much baggage, call it living and speaking *on mission* among reached peoples. But among the two callings of the Great Commission—one to disciple the reached and one the unreached—just about all the inertia in our lives and churches and communities is toward the first calling, not the second. We have no present concern in the church that too many Christians will up and move to unreached. The reached are relatively well engaged, even as great needs persist among the reached, but the unreached are in even more dire straits. *Missions* is a term for noting that difference and preserving the church's category for planting the gospel among peoples not yet reached.

Call to the Millennials

The origin of this book was in the inaugural Cross student missions conference in Louisville, Kentucky, December 27–30, 2013. The conference was a fresh effort to call college students from among the emerging Millennial generation (born 1980–2000) to the gospel frontiers for, perhaps, the last great push in the completion of the Commission.

It may sound daunting to learn that 6,500–7,000 of the world's people groups are unreached (and more than 40 percent of those are presently unengaged), but it's also deeply encouraging to put these figures into context, and see that "the momentum of closure is accelerating."[4] As missiologist Patrick Johnstone wrote more than a decade ago, "Although many people are still unreached, the number is only a fraction of that of 100 years ago. The goal is attainable in our generation—if we mobilize in prayer and effort and work together to disciple the remaining least reached peoples."[5]

Cross is one such effort to mobilize prayer and partner together in summoning a new generation not just to live on mission among our native reached peoples, and be engaged "senders," but also to be sent to the unreached and unengaged, and take up the "going" that the Commission requires. Cross aims to fly the flag for the frontier and wave the banner for *missions* and the irreplaceable, and beautiful, work of crossing cultures and learning languages to plant the gospel among those who otherwise have no access.[6]

Feet Still Matter

But to the rising generation, "going" anywhere may seem as easy, in one sense, and as unimportant as ever. In an age of increasing globalization and rapid technological advance, in which we can virtually "go" anywhere and see anything with a smart phone, a fresh localism is on the rise, and for good reason. For most of us, at least in the United States, nationalism is too big, and too disparate, to capture us for what we're missing in the Internet Age. Now we must seize upon that which is local to balance out the place-lessness we feel at work and in our social (media) lives.

But when it comes to *missions* and completing the Global Cause, feet are as important as they've ever been. Where you put your feet matters as much today as ever. With our flurry of innovations, it's easy to suppose there must be all sorts of ways in which the labor of disciplemaking, that once demanded that we be onsite, now can be done remotely. No doubt, there are a host of gains and potential assets such an age brings to world evangelization and theological education. But the computer will never replace the missionary—because the Commission doesn't call for mere exchange of information, but for good old-fashioned disciplemaking.

Discipling the nations requires more than dropping a translated tract or piping in a recording, or even a well-produced video. Disciplemaking requires more than a low-bandwidth, user-friendly website in multiple trade languages. Disciplemaking means getting your feet wet, and your whole body, in baptism, and teaching not just what Jesus commanded, but to *observe* all that he commanded (Matt. 28:19). It means doing the long-term grunt work to entrust the gospel to faithful men who will be able to teach others also (2 Tim. 2:2). It means older women training younger women holistically (Titus 2:3–5). It means being "among" the people we hope to reach with the gentleness of a nursing mother and the strength of an encouraging father (1 Thess. 2:7, 11–12). It means an eagerness to share not only the gospel, but our own selves (1 Thess. 2:8), providing a life example to imitate (Phil. 3:17), and empowering the disciples to practice what they have learned and received and heard and seen in us (Phil. 4:9). Full-orbed disciplemaking cannot be accomplished remotely. It won't happen over the Internet.

And so, still at the very heart of missions is where you put your feet. Sure, there is more involved in cross-cultural missions than mere geography, but there is always some geography. There is some shared footspace. There is no disciplemaking by proxy, no distance option for finishing the mission. There is language to learn and dialects to discern and customs with which to become acquainted. And while modern transportation, unprecedented migration, and increasing globalization may make geography less a barrier than ever before, that doesn't mean that it's not still a significant barrier, and that we downplay the importance of location to our own loss and the compromise of Commission.

Disciple is Jesus' central command in Matthew 28:18–20, but *going* is inextricably linked to discipling in this context. Isaiah 52:7, quoted so memorably in Romans 10:15, is still as relevant as ever: "How beautiful are the feet of him who brings good news!" Perhaps even more so when we're faced with the location-minimizing temptations we are today. The feet of those who leave behind family and friends and familiarity to adapt to language and custom *and place* are still the most beautiful feet in the world—because they echo the journey of the nail-scarred feet that left behind heaven's everything to come to us in our nothing.

We Are Turning to the Nations

There comes a moment in every movement of God when continuing to saturate one's native people with the gospel is simply no longer enough. This is true of many in our day, who have enjoyed renewal in the fresh wave of gospel-centeredness and new depth in the soil of Reformed theology. But as the movement has grown and deepened and matured, we've increasingly felt the power of God's words through Isaiah,

> "It is too light a thing that you should be my servant to raise up the tribes of Jacob and to bring back the preserved of Israel; I will make you as a light for the nations, that my salvation may reach to the end of the earth." (Isa. 49:6)

It's not enough just to make more young, restless Reformed types among our already reached people. It is "too light a thing," as Isaiah would say, to see biblical substance and depth make a resurgence among conservative evangelicals. This vision of God is too big for a tribal deity. The God of the Scriptures is a God of the nations. The very message of such a big, gracious God is called into question if we are not soon turning to the nations.

More than one hundred years ago, in 1888, it was too small a thing for Robert Wilder and his companions at Princeton. God called them out from New England, and from the United States, to take the gospel to the unevangelized. The Student Volunteer Movement of which they became a part, sent out more than twenty thousand students in its short history.

Some eight decades before them, it was too light a thing for the renewal of the Second Great Awakening (roughly 1790–1840) to be contained among already reached peoples. In August 1806, Samuel Mills and fellow students of Williams College experienced the so-called "Haystack Meeting" that stirred them, and soon others, for missions, including Adoniram Judson (1788–1850), who left for Burma in early 1812.

Mills, in turn, had been inspired by William Carey (1761–1834), who is known as the father of modern missions and had felt the same restlessness and eventual call to turn to the unreached peoples beyond his homeland. For Carey it was too light a thing that God would only reach England. Now, said Carey in effect, we are turning to the nations.

But perhaps the most moving turn to the nations came in Acts 13. There Paul and his companions came to Antioch in Pisidia, and as was his practice, Paul began by evangelizing the "reached" people of the day, his fellow Jews in the synagogue. After his first message, they wanted to hear more—"the people begged that these things might be told them the next Sabbath" (Acts 13:42). But the mood changed the next week when "the whole city gathered to hear the word of the Lord" (Acts 13:44).

See if you can put yourself in the setting as a Gentile. Jew and Gentile have gathered to hear this remarkable news brought to the Jewish people. These are "things into which angels long to look" (1 Pet. 1:12), and the Gentiles stand with the angels, looking in from the outside. What an amazing thing God has done for the Jews.

When the Jewish leaders see the crowds Paul had attracted, "they were filled with jealousy and began to contradict what was spoken by Paul, reviling him" (Acts 13:45). To which Paul and Barnabas respond with this amazing statement—this turning to offer the grace of the gospel to "unclean" Gentiles. Imagine standing among your fellow Gentiles and hearing his extraordinary message of salvation, peering in from the outside on what God was offering the Jews, and then seeing Paul turn and extend this invitation to you.

> Paul and Barnabas spoke out boldly [to the Jewish leaders], saying, "It was necessary that the word of God be spoken first to you. Since you thrust it aside and judge yourselves unworthy of eternal life, behold, we are turning to the Gentiles. For so the Lord has commanded us, saying, 'I have made you a light for the Gentiles, that you may bring salvation to the ends of the earth.'" And when the Gentiles heard this, they began rejoicing and glorifying the word of the Lord, and as many as were appointed to eternal life believed. (Acts 13:46–48)

Behold, we are turning to the nations. It is too light a thing for God merely to raise up the tribes of Israel. It is too light a thing to produce a second Great Awakening at the beginning of the nineteenth century and bring renewal to America. And it is too light a thing to usher in a resurgence of big-God theology among Western evangelicals in the early twenty-first century. We are turning to the nations. The salvation of this global God must be offered to the ends of the earth.

And so comes the missions moment, that glorious pivot when we realize that the initial thrust of the movement has run its course, and it is time to truly go global with the grace we've received. When people take the Word of God seriously, there is revival among the reached and missions to the unreached. Send out the beautiful feet.

Be a World Christian

In the chapters that follow, you will be summoned, again and again, to consider the missionary call to the unreached and unengaged. We expect that many of you reading this book already embrace this call, or have begun to sense it. But what follows in these pages is not only for current and future missionaries, but for the whole church, because this Great Commission is a venture we share in together. Yes, there are two distinct callings, but there is one team, one Lord, one Great Commission. So we pray that God would use this book to solidify your current season in life, or to open new vistas on your next, and we invite you to "world Christianity"—which is really the only Christianity.

For many, we hope that will mean embracing the beautiful calling to cross cultures to bring the gospel to a people group that otherwise has no access. For others, that will mean becoming or reinforcing what it means to be an engaged *sender*—one who not only sees his own life among his native people as *sent* for evangelism, but also is actively involved in the financial and prayer support of *sending* and sustaining missionaries to the unreached.

Becoming a world Christian means that, wherever you live, you "consider all other citizenship a secondary matter"[7] and "reorder your life around God's global cause."[8] It means that even as you give yourself to making disciples on the tract of land to which you've been sent, you connect your efforts with the Global Cause, among peoples reached and unreached, and you pray and dream and give toward completing the task.

But becoming a world Christian not only leads to the resourcing and flourishing of ministries abroad; it also leads to vibrancy and fruit at home. "Becoming a world Christian cannot be an end in itself," writes Don Carson. "The aim is not to become so international and culturally flexible that one does *not* fit in anywhere; the aim, rather, is to become so understanding and flexible that one *can* soon fit in and further the gospel anywhere."[9]

Christ, Gospel, Peoples, Joy

In the chapters that follow, we will hear from a rich cross-selection of Christian leaders and missionaries. There's a Korean, a Canadian, a Zambian, some Americans, and one Malaysian-born Chinese Aussie. We have Baptists and Presbyterians, a pastor from Texas and one from Africa, and two authors of more than fifty books. There's a CEO, a university chaplain, a world-class theologian, and a seminary chancellor. We have two international college ministry leaders, one former high school basketball coach, one former mining engineer, and a former Muslim. In addition to the United States, members from our team live in Japan, Zambia, Australia, and the United Arab Emirates.

Let me warn you, and entice you, that this missions book has a lot to say about Jesus and his gospel. We do not assume the gospel and then invest our energies into statistical observations and brainstorming about strategies. We glory in the gospel, and believe that it will be men and women who glory daily in the gospel who will be most powerful in finishing the mission.

The chapters ahead will call you over and over to consider God's call in the Global Cause and to cross the line. What is he doing in and through you in the moments invested in the truths rehearsed in these chapters? Is he steadying the work of your hands on the field? Summoning you to cross over into some new venture? Inspiring you to cross from local Christian to world Christian, to take up the flag in your church for the unreached? Daring you to dream big and cross the line into the next season of your life for engaging the unengaged with the gospel? These contributors won't let you go until you've considered your calling afresh and you're ready to "go back to your life," if you go back, with renewed vigor and purpose. Or until you've resolved to be caught up into crossing the street, or crossing a border, or crossing an ocean, or crossing a culture in the call of the Commission.

The invitation is for real. Jesus will build his church; the gates of hell will not prevail against her (Matt. 16:18). The most important person alive has summoned you into the most important venture on the planet. Will you cross?

CHAPTER 1

The Chief End of Missions

The Supremacy of God in the Joy of All Peoples

═══ John Piper ═══

The Cross student missions conference, and now this book inspired by it, is a dream come true for me. And my prayer is that many of you will look back some day and see that the content captured here became a decisive moment in a dream come true for you—that some day, ten or twenty or thirty years from now, you will recall the very first Cross conference, or a word in one of these chapters, as a turning point when God did something decisive in directing the rest of your life. If you come to this book with low expectations, get big ones right now.

A Dream Come True

There are at least four reasons why first the conference, and now this book, is a dream come true for me.

1. God created the world and has been active in it from the beginning so that the transcendent beauty of his holiness might be known and enjoyed and shared by a redeemed people from every tribe and tongue and people and nation, and this book is God's work to propel that purpose toward completion. To be a part of something so central to God's ultimate purpose is what I dream about for my life.

2. The Cross conference and this book are a dream come true because every human being on this planet is lost and bound for eternal suffering unless they come to know and treasure Jesus Christ and the good news that God sent him into the world to die, and in dying to absorb and remove that judgment for everyone who believes. And the conference and this book exist to make that global human lostness—that impending eternal suffering—shockingly clear, and then propel to all the unreached peoples of the world an army of lovers who care about all human suffering, especially eternal suffering.

3. Third, the conference and book are a dream come true for me because in my lifetime God has brought about a great awakening to the glory of his sovereign grace. Call it Reformed theology. Call it the doctrines of grace. Call it the new Calvinism. Call it Big God theology. Call it a passion for God's supremacy in all things. Call it the resurgence of God-centered, Christ-exalting, Bible-saturated worship. Call it a vision of a great, holy, just, wise, good, gracious, sovereign God whose throne is established in the heavens and who does whatever he pleases. Call it what you will. God is doing this—God is awakening millions of people all over the world, especially young people—to these stunning and glorious realities. And this book is a fruit of this awakening. It is the sharpening and the pushing of the point of the spear of this gospel truth into the unreached peoples of the world, as John Stott said, "for His Imperial Majesty of Jesus Christ and for the glory of his empire."

4. Fourth, this book is a dream come true for me because I am old and I suspect that most of the readers will be young. Most of

my heroes died before they were my age—Calvin, Luther, Tyndale, Owen, Spurgeon, Edwards, Brainerd, Judson—all dead before they were sixty-seven. They didn't have this privilege at my age. Ever since God did an unusual awakening in me in 1983, when I was thirty-seven years old, I have wanted my life to count for the sake of the unreached peoples of the world. The rising of the Cross conference for students feels like a crowning gift from God—like an answer to the prayer of Psalm 71:18, "Even to old age and gray hairs, O God, do not forsake me, until I proclaim your might to another generation." God is mighty, young people. Unstoppably mighty. He will have the nations. He will have his world.

And now I get the privilege of talking to you about him under the title: "The Chief End of Missions: The Supremacy of God in the Joy of All Peoples." So this is all a dream come true. And I pray again that many of you will look back some day and see that this was the beginning of a dream come true for you. Or perhaps not the beginning but a decisive milestone, making plain what God has been doing in your life all along.

Explaining the Title

You may hear in my title a paraphrase of the first question in the Westminster Catechism:

Q. 1. What is the chief end of man?
A. Man's chief end is to glorify God, and to enjoy him forever.

So I have replaced "chief end of man" with "chief end of missions"—which seems legitimate because missions is shorthand for "man active in doing missions." There are no missions in the abstract without human action. There are only people doing missions. What is their chief end or goal? Or, what is God's chief end in their action?

Then I changed "the glory of God" to "the supremacy of God." The chief end of missions is the exaltation of God as *supremely* glorious—*supremely* beautiful and valuable above all other reality. The chief end of missions is the radical transformation of human hearts through faith in Christ and through the work of the Holy Spirit so that they treasure and magnify the glory of God *supremely* above all things. In that sense, the end of missions is the *supremacy* of God.

Then I changed "and enjoy him forever" to "the joy of all peoples." Missions is not just about winning your *neighbor* to Christ. It is about the *peoples* of the world. "Let the *peoples* praise you, O God; let all the *peoples* praise you!" (Ps. 67:3).

So the chief end of missions is *the glorification of God's supremacy in the jubilation of human hearts among all the peoples of the world.* Or we could say: the chief end of missions is the supremacy of God in the satisfaction of the peoples in God. Or, the chief end of missions is the glory of God in the God-centered gladness of the peoples.

Most Important: Changing "And" to "In"

But the most important change I made in the catechism was changing the word *and* to the word *in*. The catechism says, "Man's chief end is to glorify God, *and* to enjoy him forever." What does *and* mean? If *and* means that there is one end of man called "glorify God," and another end of man called "enjoy him forever," then why did the authors of the catechism use the singular *end* when they answered, "The chief *end* of man is . . ."? Why didn't they say, "The chiefs *ends* of man *are* to glorify God and enjoy him forever"?

The answer is that the authors did *not* consider God's getting glory in man and man's getting joy in God as separate and distinct *ends*. They knew that God's being glorified in us and our being satisfied in him were one thing.

One thing—the way God looking stunning through me is one thing with my being stunned by him. He looks stunning *in* my being stunned. God's being glorified and my enjoying him is one thing the way God looking ravishing is one thing with my being ravished. God's being glorified and my enjoying him are one thing the way God looking like the supreme treasure over all is one thing with my treasuring him as the supreme treasure over all. The world sees the supreme value of God in our valuing him supremely.

Those great Reformed theologians of the seventeenth century knew that God's being glorified in us and our being satisfied in him were not two separate goals of creation. They were one goal, one end. And so they wrote, "The chief *end* (not ends) of man is to glorify God and enjoy him forever." And what I am doing is simply making it explicit and clear *how* they are one in my paraphrase: "The chief end of missions is the supremacy of God *in* the joy of all peoples"— namely, the joy of all peoples in God.

When the peoples of the earth come to rejoice supremely in the Lord, the Lord will be supremely glorified in the peoples of the earth. There is one end, one aim, one goal, of missions: the full and everlasting gladness of the peoples in the glory of God. Or, the glorification of God in the full and everlasting gladness of the peoples in God.

What does this most important change from "and" to "in" imply for your motivation in missions? The change from "The chief end of missions is the supremacy of God *and* the joy of all peoples" to "The chief end of missions is the supremacy of God *in* the joy of all peoples"—why does that matter for you? For your motivation in reading this book? For being open to God's leading in your life in regard to the unreached peoples of the world?

The reason it matters is because this change (from "and" to "in") clarifies the relationship between the two great biblical motivations for doing missions: the joy you have in *seeing God glorified*, and the joy you have in *seeing people saved*—passion for the supremacy of God and compassion for perishing people.

Which do you have? Which is driving you? God's glory or man's good? God's worth or man's rescue? God's holiness or man's happiness? The exaltation of God's supremacy or the salvation of man's soul? What is your driving missions motivation?

Why the Change Matters

The main reason it matters that I have changed "the supremacy of God *and* the joy of all peoples" to "the supremacy of God *in* the joy of all peoples," is that this makes it clear you don't have to choose between those two motives. In fact, you dare not choose. If you choose between them, both are cancelled. They live and die together. Rightly understood these two motives are one and not two.

When we say, "The chief end of missions is the supremacy of God *in* the joy of all peoples," we make plain that zeal for the supremacy of God *includes* a zeal for the joy of all peoples. And the other way around, compassion on the joyless eternity of lost peoples *includes* a zeal for the glory of God. Rightly understood, it cannot be otherwise.

These are not separate motives, as if missions could be pursued with a zeal for the glory of God, but no zeal for the joy of lost people! Or as if missions could be pursued with a zeal for the joy of the lost, but no zeal for the glory of God. No, that's not possible. Indifference to the glorification of God *is* indifference to the eternal joy of the peoples. Indifference to the eternal joy of the peoples is indifference to the glory of God. Because missions aims at the supremacy of God *in* the joy of all peoples—the joy of the peoples *in* God.

To be sure, not all people will be saved. Not all will enjoy God forever. Many will hate him to eternity. And God will glorify his holy wrath in their righteous judgment. But that is *not* the goal of missions. Missions is a rescue movement to glorify God in the gladness of the peoples.

These are not two separate motives. They are one. "The chief end of missions is the supremacy of God *in*—not *and*—the joy of all peoples." You don't have to answer the question, "Which is driving you? God's glory or man's good? God's worth or man's rescue? God's holiness or man's happiness? The exaltation of God's supremacy or the salvation of man's soul?"

Stated like that, there is no right answer to that question. This *or* that. No. Not: this *or* that; but: this *in* that. Not "God's glory *or* man's joy"; but: "God's glory revealed *in* man's joy"—man's joy *in* *God*. Not: God's worth *or* man's rescue; but God's worth revealed *in* man's rescue—his rescue from the deadly condition of not treasuring God's worth. God's worth is magnified when a person flees from a lifetime of belittling God's worth.

So you dare not choose between being motivated by your compassion for lost people and your zeal for the glory of God. If you know what the glory of God is, and you know what it means to be rescued from sin, then you will know that you must have *both* motives because they are one. The glory of God in the gladness of the peoples, and the gladness of the peoples in the glory of God.

The Bible's Pervasive Message: God's Glory

Let's go to the Bible now and see if these things are so. Perhaps here is where the Holy Spirit will put the match to the kindling I am trying to lay.

The uniform and pervasive message of the Bible is that all things have been done *by God* for the glory of God, and all things should, therefore, be done *by us* for the glory of God. This doesn't mean we do them to *increase* his glory, but to *display* his glory. To *communicate* his glory—the supreme beauty of his manifold perfections.

The apostle Paul comes to the end of the great explanation of redemptive history in Romans 9–11 and writes in Romans 11:36, "From him and through him and *to him* are all things. *To him* be glory forever."

"*To him* are all things." All things exist to him, that is, to his honor, to his fame, for the sake of his name and his praise. All things—absolutely all things, from microwave ovens to global missions, from the tiniest microbe to human cultures, all things are "to him." To him be glory forever. All the peoples, all the languages, all the tribes are *to him*. They exist for him. His name, his praise, his honor, his glory.

Paul says again in Colossians 1:16, "All things were created through him and *for him*," referring to Christ. Everything in creation exists *for him*. For the honor of Christ, for the glory of Christ. For the name and the fame of Christ (cf. Heb. 2:10).

Or again in Romans 1:5, Paul says, "We have received grace and apostleship to bring about the obedience of faith *for the sake of [Christ's] name* among all the nations." "For the sake of Christ's name." Paul's apostleship, and by extension the cause of missions, and this conference, exist "for the sake of Christ's name among all the nations." For the name and honor and glory and fame of Jesus Christ.

This is where John Stott says in his commentary on Romans that the mission of the church exists "for His Imperial Majesty, Jesus Christ, and for the glory of his empire." For all we know, America may be a footnote in the history of the world someday, and every President virtually forgotten, just like the Caesars of Rome—how many Caesars can you name? (There were eighty.) But we know beyond all doubt that the name and the majesty and the kingdom of Christ, in the words of Daniel the prophet, "shall never be destroyed. . . . It shall break in pieces all these kingdoms and bring them to an end, and it shall stand forever" (Dan. 2:44).

The point of all these texts—and dozens more like them—is that God's aim in creation is to put himself on display and to magnify the greatness of his glory. "The heavens are telling of the glory of God" (Ps. 19:1 NASB). He designed it that way. That is what the galaxies are for. And that is what everything that happens in creation is for. All of history, from creation to consummation, exists for the communication of the glory of God.

Isaiah 48:9–11 flies like a banner not just over God's rescue of Israel from exile, but over all his acts of rescue, especially the cross of Christ:

> For my name's sake I defer my anger, for the sake of my praise I restrain it for you, that I may not cut you off. Behold, . . . I have tried you in the furnace of affliction. For my own sake, for my own sake, I do it, for how should my name be profaned? My glory I will not give to another.

All of creation, all of redemption, all of history is designed by God to display God—to magnify the greatness of the glory of God. That is the ultimate goal, all things, including missions. "The chief end of missions is the supremacy of God—the display and communication of the supreme worth and beauty of God."

Another Stream of Revelation: Our Gladness

But there is another stream of revelation flowing in the Bible concerning what God is up to in the world he has made and the world he is governing. He is not only seeking the glorification of his name; he is seeking the jubilation of the peoples *in* his name. Ponder this second stream of texts with me for a few moments.

Paul tells us in Romans 15:8 that the Son of God came to confirm God's promises to the Jews. But immediately, then, he adds in verse 9, "and in order that the Gentiles"—the non-Jewish peoples of the world—"might glorify God for his mercy." And then he tells us what it means to glorify God for his mercy—his mercy! He quotes four Old Testament passages about God's purpose for the joy of the nations (Rom. 15:9–12):

> As it is written, "Therefore I will *praise* you among the Gentiles, and *sing* to your name." And again it is said, "*Rejoice,* O Gentiles, with his people." And again, "*Praise* the Lord, all you Gentiles, and let all the peoples *extol* him." And again Isaiah says, "The root of Jesse will come, even he who arises to rule the Gentiles; in him will the Gentiles *hope*."

What does it mean that God's aim in missions is "that the Gentiles might glorify God for his mercy"? Gather up all his words! It means, Let the peoples *praise*! Let the peoples *sing*! Let the peoples *rejoice*! Let the peoples *extol*! Let the peoples *hope*! It is unmistakable what God is up to in history: the gladness of the peoples in God!

And if we go back to the Psalms, the purpose of God for all the peoples of the earth is clear: joy in God above all things.

- Psalm 47:1: "Clap your hands, all peoples! Shout to God with loud songs of joy!"
- Psalm 66:1–2: "Shout for joy to God, all the earth; sing the glory of his name; give to him glorious praise!"
- Psalm 67:3–4: "Let the peoples praise you, O God; let all the peoples praise you! Let the nations be glad and sing for joy."
- Psalm 68:32: "O kingdoms of the earth, sing to God; sing praises to the Lord."
- Psalm 96:1: "Oh sing to the Lord a new song; sing to the Lord, all the earth!"
- Psalm 97:1: "The Lord reigns, let the earth rejoice; let the many coastlands be glad!"

- Psalm 98:4: "Make a joyful noise to the Lord, all the earth; break forth into joyous song and sing praises!"
- Psalm 100:1: "Make a joyful noise to the Lord, all the earth!"

There is no doubt that God's global aim in creation and redemption is not only the glory of his name but also the gladness of the peoples. Specifically, the gladness of the peoples *in God*.

And if someone asks, Couldn't you do the same thing with faith and obedience and life? Couldn't you trace through all the Bible the places where God aims at these? Why not focus on those as the aim of God and the aim of missions?

If you ask that, I would say, Why do you think the great theologians who wrote the Westminster Catechism said, "The chief end of man is to glorify God and *enjoy* him forever"? Why didn't they say, "To glorify God and *trust* him forever"? Or, "To glorify God and *obey* him forever"? Or, "To glorify God and have *life* in him forever"?

Isn't the answer that the essence of each of these experiences—of faith and obedience and life, indeed all genuine spiritual experience—isn't the essence of them all the enjoyment of God *in* those acts, such that if you remove the enjoyment of God from them (faith, obedience, life), they cease to be God-exalting acts?

- Isn't the essence of faith the embrace of God in Christ as the all-sufficient satisfier of our souls—not just the giver of good gifts, but the giver himself? Isn't faith, at its essence, being satisfied with all that God is for us in Jesus (John 6:35)?
- And isn't obedience, with all its thousands of manifestations, at its essence, doing what God says with a view to enjoying more of God in the very doing of it, and the reward of it? For example, we obey the command to love our neighbor by expanding our joy in God in our neighbor's enjoyment of

God. I would argue that this is the nature of all God-exalting obedience (cf. Heb. 12:2; Acts 20:35; 2 Cor. 9:7).

- And isn't the essence of eternal life to know God, as Jesus says in John 17:3? And what is knowing God in the fullest biblical sense? To know him like the devil knows him, with all the facts just right, but hating them? No. To know God in a saving way is to know his all-satisfying beauty and greatness and worth for what they really are, precious and soul-satisfying. To know him rightly is to treasure what is known.

If the enjoyment of God is withdrawn as an essential aspect of faith or obedience or life, they cease to be the goal of God. They cease to be what they are. Faith is not saving faith without being satisfied in all that God is for us in Christ. Obedience is not obedience where there's no obedience to the command, "Rejoice in the Lord always" (Phil. 4:4). And life is not life where God himself is not our delight.

So I say again, in creation and redemption and in the mission of the church, God aims supremely at both: the glory of his name, and the gladness of the peoples.

Why Jesus Came

And in the fullness of time, the Son of God, Jesus Christ, came into the world to secure both of these goals. He came for the vindication of his Father's glory, and for the salvation of his Father's children. And he did this by dying on the cross and rising from the dead.

The night before he died, in great distress he said, "What shall I say? 'Father, save me from this hour'? But for this purpose I have come to this hour. Father, glorify your name." Then a voice came from heaven: "I have glorified it, and I will glorify it again" (John 12:27–28). Christ died for glory-belittling sinners to show that God does not sweep the dishonoring of his name under the rug of the universe. He died to vindicate the worth of his glory (Rom. 3:23–26).

And he also came "to seek and to save the lost" (Luke 19:10). He said, "The Son of Man came . . . to give his life as a ransom for many" (Mark 10:45). A ransom from everlasting misery to everlasting joy—"These things I have spoken to you, that my joy may be in you, and that your joy may be full" (John 15:11; cf. 17:13). And at the end of the age, when all the peoples are gathered before Jesus, those who have received him as their treasure will hear the words, "Enter into the joy of your master" (Matt. 25:23). This is why he came: to purchase by his blood the joy of the peoples in the joy of their Master.

Jesus died for this: the glory of his Father, and the gladness of his people. Frontier missions is an extension to the nations of Jesus' mission to the world. He came for the glory of the Father and the gladness of the peoples. So the chief end of missions is the supremacy of God *and* the joy of all peoples.

But not just *and*, rather *in*. The aim of history, the aim of Christ in dying for sinners is the glory of God *in* the gladness of the nations. The chief end of missions is the supremacy of God *in* the joy of all peoples.

This is so because when you enjoy someone you honor that person. You magnify their value. You glorify them. If I say to my wife, "It makes me happy to be with you," she doesn't accuse me of selfishness. Why? I just said that I am motivated to be with her by my own happiness. Because when my happiness is in her, it calls attention to her worth, not mine. She is honored when I say, "It makes me happy to be with you." So is Christ. So is God the Father. They are seen to be a supreme treasure when they become for us our supreme pleasure. They are glorified in us when we are satisfied in them.

Embrace the One Great End

Therefore I say again, "The chief end of missions is the supremacy of God *in* the joy of all peoples." When the peoples find their supreme gladness in God, God will be supremely glorified in them. Which is why he created the world, and why Jesus' cross exist, and that's why the Cross conference and this book exist. That's what we pray will be the everlasting upshot of those days and these pages.

We will not choose between glorifying God and making people glad. We will not choose between praising God's supremacy and removing people's suffering—especially eternal suffering. We will not choose between hallowing God and helping people. In the aims of the Cross conference, and the aims of global missions, we will not choose between the aim of seeing Christ magnified among the peoples and seeing the peoples satisfied in Christ.

Because these two are one. Christ is supremely magnified in the peoples when the peoples are supremely satisfied in Christ. We have the best news in all the world: Jesus Christ, the Son of God, died and rose and reigns to make the nations fully and eternally glad in the glory of God.

When Christ becomes the satisfaction of the nations, and God becomes their delight, then he is honored and they are saved. And you—you who will take or send this best of all messages—you turn out to be a person of great compassion toward perishing sinners and great zeal for the glory of God. Don't ever choose between these two: praising God and pitying sinners, divine glory and human gladness. Embrace this one great end, and give your life to it—the supremacy of God in the joy of all peoples.

CHAPTER 2

Beauty from Ashes

The Plight of Man and the Plan of God

Thabiti Anyabwile

I do not want you to be unaware, brothers, that I have often intended to come to you (but thus far have been prevented), in order that I may reap some harvest among you as well as among the rest of the Gentiles. I am under obligation both to Greeks and to barbarians, both to the wise and to the foolish.

So I am eager to preach the gospel to you also who are in Rome. For I am not ashamed of the gospel, for it is the power of God for salvation to everyone who believes, to the Jew first and also to the Greek. For in it the righteousness of God is revealed from faith for faith, as it is written, "The righteous shall live by faith." For the wrath of God is revealed from heaven against all ungodliness and unrighteousness of men, who by their unrighteousness suppress the truth.

(Rom. 1:13–18)

In these six verses of Scripture, we find a more complete statement of this chapter's subtitle. Here in this passage is both the plan of God (vv. 13–17) and the plight of man (v. 18). If we were to summarize this text in one overarching thought, we might put it this way: *The plan of God is to send unashamed preachers to reach unreached peoples to display his unparalleled power and unearned righteousness in saving from an unrelenting wrath.*

The Plan of God

This plan must be carried out in a certain way.

First, we pursue the plan with the correct motivation. In verse 15, Paul says, "I am eager . . ." He's eager. He has a keen interest. He has an intense desire or a restless expectation. Paul is like a dog pulling hard on his master's leash trying to chase every animal with the bark of the gospel. He's straining forward in the gospel.

And why shouldn't he be eager? The gospel is the best news in the universe! There ought to be in us the same eagerness, zeal, and burning to herald this happy news. We should be dogs pulling on our Master's leash, barking to make Christ known—eager, anticipating, desirous that our Lord's glory should be known.

So we ought to ask ourselves: Am I eager? Am I eager to play my part in the plan of God to reach the nations? We must pursue God's plan with eagerness.

Second, we pursue the plan with the correct method—"preach the gospel." The plan of God is that by the foolishness of preaching, men and women will hear the message that rescues them. The gospel must be taught before it is caught. Christ must be proclaimed if he is going to be possessed. There must be the use of words if men will ever know the wonder of God's love for a sinful world.

When Paul boils down his missionary method to its bedrock foundation, he always talks of preaching and teaching the gospel.

He builds everything—his entire missionary agenda—on this one essential method. So Paul says things like, "I decided to know nothing among you except Jesus Christ and him crucified" (1 Cor. 2:2). Or, "Him we proclaim, warning everyone and teaching everyone with all wisdom, that we may present everyone mature in Christ" (Col. 1:28).

That's his method. I emphasize this for one reason: too many Christians wrongly think Christ can be made known without the use of words. That's false. And too many missionaries give so much time to strategies for getting in and remaining in countries that they sadly never get around to proclaiming Christ.

Let me be clear: missionary strategy has its place. It's essential. There are tons of things to consider when going to the hardest-to-reach places, often among the most resistant people. Strategy has a necessary place. But strategy never saved anyone. The gospel does. So all our strategy must aim at the preaching of the gospel. Strategy must position us to proclaim. We undertake every strategy in order to herald Christ. And we risk everything else in order to make Christ known.

I am not trying to be trite about the risks of serving in some places among some peoples. Many have given their lives in this cause. We are not being flippant about the need for strategy and the risks involved; we are saying that all of the scheming and calculated risks happen for another great thing to happen—the preaching, the proclaiming of the good news of Jesus Christ. That is what is uppermost in Paul's mind. Our strategy will support our preaching if we're *eager* to preach Christ.

Third, we have to pursue the plan with the correct mark—the correct aim or target. Paul wants to preach the gospel to "you also who are in Rome." Paul tells us throughout this letter that he wants to preach the gospel to people who do not know him and do not know Christ.

According to verse 13, Paul has never visited Rome or preached the gospel among the Romans because he has been laboring in other places where Christ is not named. Paul feels this obligation to Greeks and to Barbarians (v. 14). I remember Mark Dever recounting that he once heard John Stott powerfully point out from this text how Paul understood himself to have received from God an obligation for other people. May the obligation of this text rest upon our shoulders also. May God in heaven oblige us to serve not ourselves, but to serve our God and his Christ in the seeking of the nations.

This is what Paul is about. Paul hears from people in Rome, and he immediately thinks, "This is a gospel opportunity." The Romans are Gentiles with a very different world and life-view. The Romans are a people who value military might. Rome was the cosmopolitan center of the world. They were pagans who worshiped the emperor as a god and participated in a number of idolatrous temple cults.

What Paul sees when he considers the Romans is a people in need of the gospel. What we observe in this text is a Jewish man desiring to cross cultural and ethnic lines to make the gospel known to a specific people group unknown to him.

Paul is the kind of Christian who labors *most* where Christ is known *least*. So he writes in Romans 15:20–21, "I make it my ambition to preach the gospel, not where Christ has already been named, lest I build on someone else's foundation, but as it is written, 'Those who have never been told of him will see, and those who have never heard will understand.'"

If the apostle Paul were alive today and were invited to write a chapter on missions in a book like this one, I believe he would indeed address the subject of unreached and unengaged peoples. He would bring to our attention the *unreached*, those six-thousand-plus people groups with less than two percent of their population known to be Christian. He would call to mind those people groups who have no viable evangelical church among them. He would point even more specifically to the *unengaged* peoples and challenge the church to pursue those groups among which there are currently no known efforts to bring the gospel.

Paul says in chapter 15 that he wants to preach "not where Christ has already been named," but deliver the message to "those who have never been told of Jesus so they will see him and those who have never heard so they will understand." The apostle puts the entire world in the crosshairs of the gospel. We're seeing Paul for the great cross-cultural, gospel-preaching, church-planting missionary that he is. And in Paul, we're seeing a vision for what we should be about as individual Christians and together as the church.

Is this your vision for how you're going to invest your life? Are you eager? Are you feeling the need to be eager? Are you desiring to preach Christ, to make him known where he is not known? Is your heart set yet on a particular people, unreached and unengaged?

The Grounds of Paul's Ministry: Why God's Plan Is Bound to Be Successful

Why would Paul express such eagerness to preach the gospel among the Romans, among a people unknown to him and largely unknown to Jesus?

He gives us the reasons in verses 16–17. Notice the word "for" occurs three times in these two verses. That little word alerts us to the fact that Paul will now give us the reason or basis for what he states in verse 15. In this case, these three clauses tell us why Paul is so eager to preach the gospel to the Romans and why God's plan for the nations will prevail.

First, Paul is eager to preach the gospel to a people unknown to him and largely unknown to Christ because he is "not ashamed of the gospel." Paul's being unashamed releases his eagerness. We are not eager about things that embarrass us, are we? But because he is unashamed, Paul is free to be fully vested and eager to herald the good news. How did Paul become unashamed?

Paul tells us, *second*, he is not ashamed of the gospel because the gospel "is the power of God for salvation." Why be ashamed of something that contains divine power? Why be embarrassed about a message that raises dead men to life? The power of God in the gospel makes Paul barrel-chested and lionhearted. Paul has tasted and seen and felt the demonstration of the power of God in the gospel. Consequently, Paul is unashamed. And because he's unashamed, he's eager.

Third, Paul tells us the gospel is the power of God for salvation because in the gospel "the righteousness of God is revealed from faith for faith." The gospel goes out, dead men are regenerated and brought to life, given the gifts of repentance and faith; and in that faith, as they treasure and lay hold to Christ, God declares them "righteous," "justified." All that Jesus Christ is and all that he has done has become theirs by faith and the believer's union with him.

This series of *for* clauses forms a kind of chain reaction. Because Paul is confident of the power of the gospel, he is then unashamed. Because he is unashamed, he is eager. The series of clauses in these two verses is like a relay of explosive charges firing one after another. They're like bombs exploding in sequence and destroying indifference, apathy, and shame.

So, if we are ashamed or uneager, then somewhere this chain reaction has misfired. We've either failed to understand the righteousness of God revealed in the gospel or the power of God to save or the boldness that comes from a preaching ministry resting on God's power. If we're not eager to preach the gospel to the nations, then we need to find out which bomb has not exploded in our thinking and our affections—and we need to light the fuse!

This is God's plan: *to send unashamed preachers to reach unengaged peoples with God's unparalleled power and unearned righteousness in salvation.*

The Plight of Man (v. 18)

Why would such a plan be necessary? Why does God call Paul, and call us, to go to people unknown to us and unknown to Christ to preach the gospel?

Notice that verse 18 begins with "for" as well. This little word is there for two reasons.

First, the word for *explains why the righteous live by faith.* The righteous must live by faith because all other means of attempting to live before God end in the wrath of God. "For the wrath of God is revealed from heaven against all ungodliness and unrighteousness of men, who by their unrighteousness suppress the truth" (v. 18). Without the righteousness of God in the gospel, man is left attempting a righteousness of his own. But Isaiah 64:6 tells us very plainly, "We have all become like one who is unclean, and all our righteous deeds are like a polluted garment" or "filthy rags." Before an infinitely holy God, and without faith, our very best efforts at cleanness are filthy. They are merely failed attempts at self-justification. It means that when we're trying to be good *in order to be justified,* all we end up doing is making God angry. We need a righteousness from outside ourselves. That's why Paul explains in verse 18 that the righteous shall live by faith, *because* "God's wrath is being revealed against the ungodliness and unrighteousness of men."

The second reason Paul begins with wrath is because Paul is not ashamed of the gospel. Because he's not ashamed of the gospel, Paul is not ashamed of one essential doctrine of the gospel—God's wrath. Paul smoothly moves from justification by faith to devastation by wrath without self-consciousness, hand-wringing, squirming, or apologizing. Paul is not ashamed of the biblical truth that God is a God of wrath toward sinners. In fact, all the writers of the Bible are unashamed of God's wrath.

In his commentary on Romans, Jim Boice writes regarding this verse,

> Today's preaching is deficient at many points. But there is no point at which it is more evidently inadequate and even explicitly contrary to the teachings of the New Testament than in its neglect of "the wrath of God." God's wrath is a dominant Bible teaching and the point in Romans at which Paul begins his formal exposition of the gospel. Yet, to judge from most contemporary forms of Christianity, the wrath of God is either an unimportant doctrine, which is an embarrassment, or an entirely wrong notion, which any enlightened Christian should abandon.[10]

In other words, here is one place where so many Christians—even preachers and missionaries—depart tragically from the Scriptures, and it is a truth integral to the gospel. Think about those times when you've spoken with your unbelieving classmate or professor about the gospel. When God's wrath comes up, perhaps you've felt a temptation to shrink back, to try to make God a good guy in their eyes, and talk about God in a way that assures our unbelieving friend they're going to like him. How tempting it is in those times to slide over the Bible's teaching about the wrath of God.

But God is not embarrassed about his wrath. He's not ashamed of his judgment. He doesn't shrink back or try to present a more flattering side of his character while hiding behind his back a truth unpleasant to our increasingly post-Christian society. He tells us very plainly that he is a God of wrath. Not the out-of-control anger and lashing vengeance of men. His wrath is his settled, purposeful, righteous indignation or anger or fury—as verse 18 says—against the unrighteousness and ungodliness of men. In other words, God is right to be wrathful given the sins of men against his glory and goodness. His wrath is just. John Frame writes this helpful bit of instruction:

> No one should try by some exegetical or theological trick to mitigate against the harshness of this doctrine. That harshness is the whole point. To be separate from God, from his inheritance, from his people, and to be under his wrath forever is terrible to contemplate.[11]

We do some of our best work in evangelism when we make sure people understand the wrath of God against them, that their plight is desperate because God is angry. The problem of unreached and unengaged peoples is not that they don't have the gospel—that's the solution. Their plight is that they face a God who is rightly angry with them because of their sin.

We bear the Christian message best when we embrace the righteous wrath of God as good and beautiful just as we embrace his love as good and beautiful. The wrath of God is one of his perfections too. So the Christian missionary is one who worships and weeps simultaneously. We have this strange kind of embrace where, on the one hand, we exalt God for his righteousness expressed sometimes in his wrath while we, on the other hand, weep for the nations in danger of his coming wrath. Both the worship and the weeping motivate us to go and proclaim that one Savior who assuages or turns away the Father's wrath.

If we mitigate the harshness of God's wrath, we will minimize the urgency of God's mission. Leave it "harsh" or sharp or weighty because only then will we begin to understand the plight of mankind, and the serious danger unreached and unengaged peoples face because the wrath of God abides on them.

The Definition of God's Wrath

The wrath of God is related to three other attributes of God: righteousness, holiness, and justice. Martyn Lloyd-Jones writes, "The righteousness of God is God's love for holiness, and the justice of God is God's abomination of sin." God loves holiness and hates sin. The expression of those two things is wrath. Wrath is how God punishes evil and honors purity.

John Murray says, "Wrath is the holy revulsion of God's being against that which is evil arising out of God's very nature."[12] In other words, wrath is *in* God. It is part of his nature and being. His whole person is against sin and ungodliness. So, verse 18: "The wrath of God . . . *against* all ungodliness and unrighteousness of men . . ." Man's predicament is that his sin has provoked an omnipotent and holy God. God stands against man. This is why the Bible warns, "It is a fearful thing to fall into the hands of the living God" (Heb. 10:31), and, our "God is a consuming fire" (Deut. 4:24; Heb. 12:29).

Some people will object to this view of God. They say, "If God is wrathful, then he is a monster. Doesn't this make God capricious and mean?" They say, "Such anger is not consistent with a god of love." So they reject this view of God, and they try to explain away passages like Romans 1. They find this doctrine an embarrassment, unworthy of God.

But we might ask such a person a couple of questions. First, "Does evil really exist in the world in which we live?" Obviously, yes. Well, second: "Should that evil go unpunished?" Obviously, not. Then, third: "Who will punish the evil that's really in the world if not God?" Who knows how best to punish evil if not God? Finally, "What would God be like if he did not hate and punish evil and sin?" The wrath of God is as necessary a doctrine in a fallen, evil world as is the love of God.

Man wants a world where evil does not exist and where God does not punish it. But evil *does* exist. So mankind cannot have it both ways. We cannot have a world where evil is punished *and* a world where God does not punish it. God will show the perfection of his character even in the wrath shown toward evil.

The Disclosure of God's Wrath Now

Not only is God's wrath a central theme in the Bible, and the bad news that makes the good news good, but God's wrath is *a present reality*. "The wrath of God is revealed," or as some translations read, "is being revealed" (v. 18 NIV). The verb is present tense. God is right now displaying his wrath against the ungodly and the unrighteous.

Jim Boice writes, "In the Old Testament more than twenty words are used to refer to God's wrath. There are nearly six hundred important passages on the subject."[13] This is a central teaching of the Bible. God displays his wrath not only at the end of time, but also in the progress of time. Consider a few of the many Old Testament passages.

Exodus 22:23–24 provides laws about social justice for sojourners, widows, and orphans. The Lord God speaks through Moses, saying, "If you do mistreat them, and they cry out to me, I will surely hear their cry, and *my wrath will burn*, and I will kill you with the sword, and your wives shall become widows and your children fatherless."

Exodus 32:9–10 includes the famous scene where Aaron fashions the golden calf and Israel commits idolatry with it. The Lord says to Moses, "I have seen this people, and behold, it is a stiff-necked people. Now therefore let me alone, *that my wrath may burn hot against them and I may consume them*, in order that I may make a great nation of you." If Moses had not interceded for Israel, the Lord would have consumed them.

Numbers 16:43–46 recounts Israel's grumbling after God opened the earth to swallow Korah and all those who rebelled. "And Moses and Aaron came to the front of the tent of meeting, and the LORD spoke to Moses, saying, 'Get away from the midst of this congregation, that I may consume them in a moment.' And they fell on their faces. And Moses said to Aaron, 'Take your censer, and put fire on it from off the altar and lay incense on it and carry it quickly to the congregation and make atonement for them, *for wrath has gone out from the LORD*; the plague has begun.'"

Numbers 25 includes the passage where Phinehas honors the Lord by putting to death an Israelite man and Moabite woman who profaned the camp of the Lord in sexual immorality. We read: "Phinehas the son of Eleazar, son of Aaron the priest, has *turned back my wrath from the people of* Israel, in that he was jealous with my jealousy among them, so that I did not consume the people of Israel in my jealousy" (Num. 25:11).

Deuteronomy 9:7–8 says, "Remember and do not forget how you *provoked the LORD your God to wrath in the wilderness.* From the day you came out of the land of Egypt until you came to this place, you have been rebellious against the LORD. Even at Horeb *you provoked the LORD to wrath, and the LORD was so angry with you that he was ready to destroy you.*"

Joshua 22:20 refers to the cursed thing at Ai when it asks, "Did not Achan the son of Zerah break faith in the matter of the devoted things, *and wrath fell upon all the congregation of Israel*? And he did not perish alone for his iniquity."

In 2 Kings 22:13, young King Josiah finds the scroll and reads the Word of God. He laments, "Go, inquire of the LORD for me, and for the people, and for all Judah, concerning the words of this book that has been found. *For great is the wrath of the LORD that is kindled against us,* because our fathers have not obeyed the words of this book, to do according to all that is written concerning us."

Psalm 78:49–51 commemorates in song God's wrath against Egypt:

He let loose on them his burning anger,
     wrath, indignation, and distress,
     a company of destroying angels.
He made a path for his anger;
     he did not spare them from death,
     but gave their lives over to the plague.
He struck down every firstborn in Egypt,
     the firstfruits of their strength in the tents of Ham.

Beloved, these texts represent a small sampling of the Bible's texts on God's wrath. We don't have time to talk of the flood of Noah, when in his wrath against the continual wickedness of men, God destroyed all but eight souls. We don't have time to retell the story of Sodom and Gomorrah, cities whose wickedness reached heaven and God destroyed all but three souls. Or the wilderness wandering where God wiped out an entire generation of Israel, and only two souls entered the Promised Land. Or Nadab and Abihu consumed by God for offering strange fire and being consumed for doing so. Or the prophets' frequent mention of the day of the Lord when God's wrath shall burn against the nations. As J. I. Packer put it, "One of the most striking things about the Bible is the vigor with which both testaments emphasize the reality and terror of God's wrath."[14]

And most of these judgments were against his (old) covenant people! If judgment begins with the household of God, what will be the outcome for those who do not obey the gospel of our Lord (1 Pet. 4:17)? What will be the outcome for North Africa and the people groups there? What will be the outcome for the various regions of

Asia where people do not know the name of Christ? If judgment begins at the household of God, what will be the outcome for people in various lands across the planet who have yet to bow the knee in loving worship of Christ?

Psalm 76:7 proclaims:

> But you, you are to be feared!
>   Who can stand before you
>   when once your anger is roused?

Romans 1:18 tells us God's anger is already roused. No one can stand in his presence if he holds their sins against them. No one can survive—unless his wrath is turned away.

The Destruction of God's Wrath Eternally

The wrath of God revealed now in this life is only a preview of the full and final wrath of God poured out in eternity. Here's how Paul puts it in Romans 2:5: "Because of your hard and impenitent heart you are storing up wrath for yourself on the day of wrath when God's righteous judgment will be revealed." That is what is happening even while you are reading this book. There are some six thousand unreached and three thousand unengaged people groups going about their daily lives storing up wrath each hour.

What a terrifying image this is! Picture unbelieving mankind in his sin. Their righteous deeds are filthy. Their sinful deeds are filthy. They all provoke the holy anger of God. It's like making continual deposits in the First Bank of Wrath. They are storing up anger. It's like taking a day's living in the form of grain and storing it in the warehouse of God's righteous indignation. God's judgment is being built up like floods behind a dam. A trickle comes out here and there as God gives them over to their sinful desires (Rom. 1:24–28). But his full fury is being built up until the Day of Judgment when the dam shall burst and the righteous wrath of God shall sweep across the globe.

That's what happens if we don't go. Real people face the real anger of God.

The first time I saw my father in a church was at his funeral. As far as I know, he never came to faith in Christ. I loved my dad. He was about five-feet, ten-inches tall—a barrel-chested man. I remember when he was strong. He had muscular hands with fingers the size of Twinkies. He didn't say much. He either called me "Sport" or "Tiger." He came to all my games; he picked me up after all my practices.

He was never a believer. He was unfaithful to my mom. He was what we might call a "hustler" in terms of how he made his living in petty gambling. Later in life, my dad had a series of strokes, the last of which left him unable to speak, cloudy eyed, and out of it.

I'd only become a Christian about a year before the final stroke. At that point, I had no relationship with my father; he'd left the family when I was about thirteen years old. But my wife challenged me to be reconciled with my father. One night, over stuffed mushrooms at Bennigan's, she asked me, "What are you going to do when your father dies?" I shrugged at the question and replied, "I don't really know the man. I'm not sure I will feel anything."

But the Lord began to soften my heart. I started visiting him in the convalescence home where he stayed. He was a shell of himself, hardly there, unable to speak or communicate. I'd speak into his ear, and he'd slightly turn his head toward me. I remember the last visit whispering the gospel in his ear, not sure if he could hear me or what response would come, telling him of God's judgment and God's love and salvation through the Lord Jesus Christ.

I don't know what happened in my father's heart and soul. I know that morning in the church my heart broke with the finality of the casket being closed, of his life being ended. As far as I know, he went to eternity without Christ. He suffers the wrath of God—the righteous, the just, the holy wrath of God. My father.

When we say there are more than six thousand unreached people groups and three thousand unengaged people groups, we are referring to almost three billion people. We are referring to more than 40 percent of the world's population! Fathers, mothers, sons, and daughters going to an eternity without Jesus. The only thing that turns God's wrath away is Jesus.

Romans 3:25 says that God "put forward [Christ Jesus] as a propitiation by his blood, to be received by faith. . . ." Yes, God is angry, and he is right to be so. But the good news of the gospel is that he has done something to satisfy his anger. Specifically, God the Father has put forward Christ to die in our place, to shed his blood in order to turn away the Father's wrath from all those who believe and receive the gift of Christ's righteousness and forgiveness by faith.

So in 1 Thessalonians 5:9–10, Paul writes of those who believe, "God has not destined us for wrath, but to obtain salvation through our Lord Jesus Christ, who died for us." God has a people among all those nations whom he has not destined to wrath but has destined to faith in the Lord Jesus Christ. And they only come to faith and escape wrath if we go and proclaim the message. We want many more people in many more nations written about the way Paul writes about the Thessalonians earlier in the letter:

> For they themselves report concerning us the kind of reception we had among you, and how you turned to God from idols to serve the living and true God, and to wait for his Son from heaven, whom he raised from the dead, *Jesus who delivers us from the wrath to come.* (1 Thess. 1:9–10)

The wrath of God will cost somebody their life. It will either cost the unreached peoples their lives for eternity, or it will cost us Christians our earthly lives in missionary service.

Here's the question: Dare we be so in love with our lives in this world that we will stand back while three billion lose their souls and their lives in the world to come?

I believe it was Adrian Rogers who used to say, "The gospel is only good news if it gets there in time." The wrath of God upon the world means we need to be urgent in getting the gospel there in time.

CHAPTER 3

Five Surprising Motivations for Missions

━━ Kevin DeYoung ━━

I might as well tell you from the get-go: the five surprising motivations are the five points of Calvinism. As crazy as it may sound to some, I believe the strongest trust in God's sovereignty spurs us on to make the most costly sacrifices in world missions.

Now before I go any further, I need to address three types of people.

Those who do not like Calvinism. Please keep reading. After a little systematic theology and a little history, most of this chapter will be straight from the Bible. Be like the noble Bereans in Acts 17. Examine for yourself whether the things I'm saying are true to God's Word. Hang with me and have an open mind.

Those who know next to nothing about Calvinism. This describes a lot of people. You may be abundantly more familiar with *Calvin and Hobbes* than John Calvin (or Thomas Hobbes for that matter). You may have heard friends talking about Calvinism and Arminianism and wondered what all the fuss was about. "I don't get it. What's so bad about being from Armenia?" Well, actually, Armenians come from Armenia; Arminians are those who stand in the tradition of Jacob Arminius and reject doctrines like unconditional election and irresistible grace. If you have no idea what I'm talking about, that's okay. Keep reading. You don't have to have any background in any of these debates in order for God to use the Word to motivate you for missions.

Those who love Calvinism. Yes, it's true, I'm a Calvinist. So are many of you. I'm glad, but listen: this chapter is not entitled "Five Surprising Motivations for Feeling Superior to People Who Are Not Calvinists." Nothing is more inconsistent with the doctrines of grace than a haughty and ungracious spirit. I was a college student once too, and I went through the cage stage of Calvinism where you set people up with Romans 9 and make delicate saints weep and wail. That's not my goal in this chapter. My hope is that by looking at the Bible, you will find motivations for mission that you did not know were there.

A Little History and a Little Theology (About a Big God)

The so-called "five points of Calvinism" did not come from John Calvin, and they don't represent everything there is to know about the Reformed tradition (which has its roots in dozens of theologians, not just Calvin). The five points are found in the Canons of Dort—a series of theological statements issued from the church synod that met from November 13, 1618, to May 9, 1619, in the Dutch city of Dordrecht (or Dort for short). The synod was convened in order to respond to the teachings put forward by the followers of Jacob Arminius. The Remonstrants, as the Arminians were called, issued their five points first. Dort, in ruling against the Remonstrants, issued five points of its own. These five points were never meant to be a comprehensive summary of Reformed theology, let alone everything you need to know about the Bible. It was a particular controversy resulting in a narrow (but important) set of doctrines responding to a series of dogmatic assertions.

Many Christians know the five points of Calvinism (or the five heads of doctrine of Dort) by the acronym TULIP. Although the acronym is only a hundred years old and does not reflect the specific language or order of Dort, it provides a useful starting place for understanding the Reformed view of salvation.

T: total depravity. We are born into this world sinners through and through, dead in our trespasses, at enmity with God, and hardwired for iniquity.

U: unconditional election. In eternity past, God chose some to be saved in Christ. This exercise of divine sovereignty was not based on foreseen faith nor conditioned by anything we do or anything God knew that we would do.

L: limited atonement (also called "particular redemption" or "definite atonement"). Christ died effectively, particularly, and intentionally, for those who would believe in him. Although his death was sufficient for all, Christ's sacrifice was efficient only for the elect.

I: irresistible grace. Apart from human cooperation of any kind, the Spirit of God breathes new life into dry bones so that spiritually dead sinners can live. This act of grace is all of God and cannot be added to or resisted.

P: perseverance (or the preservation) of the saints. God keeps his own until the end, so that those who are justified will unfailingly be glorified. Once genuinely saved, always saved.

At first glance, it seems as if some of these points should work as *de*-motivators for missions. Why risk your neck for some unreached people group if Christ didn't die for many (or most, or any) of them? Why give of your time and your treasure for world evangelization if the elect are already chosen and nothing we do or don't do will change the number predetermined by God?

Outside of my study at church, my assistant has an inspiring poster hanging on the wall. Instead of one of those cheesy motivational scenes about hard work or teamwork, she has a "de-motivational" poster with a picture of a ship sinking. It's entitled "Mistakes," and the caption reads: "It could be that the purpose of your life is only to serve as a warning to others." Real inspiring, isn't it? That's how some of you may look at Calvinism and missions. Nothing seems like *less* of a motivation for missions than a firm belief in God's sovereignty in election. "If God is the decisive reason why some people believe and others do not, then God can take care of missions just fine without me. If God plans everything including who gets saved and who does not, then what is the point in giving up my comfort to go tell people about Jesus when it's already been determined whether they will believe or not?"

These are plausible sounding arguments. There is a kind of logic to them. The problem is they don't reflect *biblical* logic. It is not the way God reasons. And it's not what we've seen in church history. Believe it or not, Calvinists have been at the forefront of evangelical expansion and global missions.[15]

- John Calvin sent missionaries to Brazil. (Sadly, the team was betrayed by one of their own and died in South America.)
- John Elliott was sent to the native peoples in America in the 1600s.
- David Brainerd gave his life to evangelize the native peoples in America in the 1700s.

- Theodore Frelinghuysen, a Dutch Reformed pastor in New Jersey, was a fiery preacher who emphasized the need for conversion and served as a forerunner to the Great Awakening.
- William and Gilbert Tennent were Presbyterian pastors and prominent supporters of the Evangelical Awakening in the eighteenth century.
- Jonathan Edwards was the leading Calvinist theologian of the eighteenth century and was seen as the foremost defender and exporter of the revivals in the 1730s and 1740s.
- George Whitefield, a Reformed Anglican, was not only the most famous evangelist in the eighteenth century; he may have been the most famous person in the English-speaking world.
- William Carey, an English Calvinist and missionary to India, is considered the father of the missions movement as we know it today.
- Other Calvinists followed Carey in the next decades to bring the gospel to foreign lands: Robert Moffat and David Livingstone to Africa, Robert Morrison to China, Adoniram Judson to Burma, and Henry Martin to India and Persia.
- Samuel Zwemer, who grew up in the Dutch Reformed Church, served in Bahrain, Arabia, and Egypt. He is often known as the Apostle to Islam.

It's not an exaggeration to say Calvinists birthed the modern missions movement in the Protestant church. History shows us that a high view of God's all-determining sovereignty has not deterred Christians from going to hard places and giving their lives for the spread of the gospel.

Three Passages for Five Points

I'm a preacher and old habits die hard, so it's hard not to orga-
nize everything into three points, even when there are five points to
cover. I want to look at three sections in the Gospel of John in order
that we might see what Jesus saw about the sovereignty of God and
embrace what Jesus embraced—namely, that this glorious, necessary, risky, yet completely secure, beautiful, hopeful, and ultimately
successful cause of global missions rests on the unerring, unalterable
plan and purposes of God.

1. We Must Be Born Again (John 3:1–8)

> Now there was a man of the Pharisees named Nicodemus, a
> ruler of the Jews. This man came to Jesus by night and said to
> him, "Rabbi, we know that you are a teacher come from God,
> for no one can do these signs that you do unless God is with
> him." Jesus answered him, "Truly, truly, I say to you, unless one
> is born again he cannot see the kingdom of God." Nicodemus
> said to him, "How can a man be born when he is old? Can he
> enter a second time into his mother's womb and be born?" Jesus
> answered, "Truly, truly, I say to you, unless one is born of water
> and the Spirit, he cannot enter the kingdom of God. That which
> is born of the flesh is flesh, and that which is born of the Spirit
> is spirit. Do not marvel that I said to you, 'You must be born
> again.' The wind blows where it wishes, and you hear its sound,
> but you do not know where it comes from or where it goes. So it
> is with everyone who is born of the Spirit." (John 3:1–8)

Many of you are familiar with this story. Here you have
Nicodemus, a Pharisee. He's a smart guy. He's a leader. He's a ruler
of the Jews. He's as religious as they come. And he appears to be a

fairly good guy. Cowardly, sure, but unlike other Pharisees, he's not overtly hostile to Jesus. In fact, he seems genuinely interested to be with Jesus and learn from him. There's only one massive problem: Nicodemus is not born again. He recognizes Jesus as a teacher who has come from God. He affirms Jesus has done miracles. He affirms Jesus has power from on high. But that is not enough.

There's hardly anyone anti-Jesus in this country. In other countries, there are. But in America, almost everyone is positive about Jesus. What's not to like? He's helpful, he's loving, he's inclusive. He's a do-gooder in a bathrobe. There are plenty of people who don't like Christians or can't stand the church. But everyone likes Jesus. At least the Jesus they've made in their own image. And even if everything you know about Jesus is accurate, that's still enough. You may be favorable toward Jesus and believe true things about Jesus and still not be saved by Jesus. Nicodemus liked Jesus. But he wasn't saved, because he had not been born again.

As a teacher of the law, Nicodemus should have known that Jesus was likely referring to Ezekiel 36. We need to be cleansed with water and given a new heart by the Holy Spirit. That's called "regeneration" or "the new birth." That's what Jesus means by being born again. Titus 3:5 calls it "the washing of regeneration and renewal of the Holy Spirit." We all need a supernatural work in our sorry hearts from our sovereign God.

Jesus says, just like the wind. Just like the wind blows where it wishes, so it is with everyone born of the Spirit. The Greek word for wind and Spirit is the same: *pneuma*. The sovereign wind of God's Spirit must invade your heart and awaken you to the vileness of your sin, the truthfulness of God's Word, and the preciousness of Christ. When the Spirit causes us to be born again, we will be irrevocably changed. A profession of faith that makes no difference in us will make no difference to God either. There is no Christian life without the converting work of the Spirit. Because apart from this work,

we're lost in sin, dead in trespasses, spiritually lifeless, unable, inca-
pable, defiled, and depraved.

The language of total depravity does not mean that we are absolutely as bad as we possibly could be. Praise God for common grace.
If you meet a stranger walking into school, he's more likely to hold
the door for you than shove you to the ground. Non-Christians can
be kind, decent people. But in an ultimate sense, we cannot do anything morally praiseworthy unless the Spirit of God gives us the
right motivation and the right heart. The word *total* refers to the
extent of our depravity. We are not just bent toward evil in our appe-
tites or base faculties. We are also depraved in mind and will. Every
part of us—our reason, our intellect, our affections—is all inclined
toward God-denying, idolatry-creating, truth-suppressing sin. "Are
we so corrupt that we are totally unable to do any good and inclined
toward all evil?" asks the Heidelberg Catechism. Answer: "Yes,
unless we are born again by the Spirit of God" (Q/A 8).

Isn't that what Jesus is saying? That you will not see the kingdom of God, that will you not go to heaven, that you will not live
forever unless you are born again supernaturally, sovereignly, by the
Spirit of God? If you really believe we are inclined toward evil, if you
really believe no one is righteous (Rom. 3:10), if you really believe we
are born in this world dead in our trespasses and by nature children
of wrath (Eph. 2:1–4), then we are going to see this world and its
plight in a very different way from many of our friends.

Every year around Christmas my wife likes to watch a film
adaptation of Dickens's *A Christmas Carol*. It's a wonderful story in
many ways, but like so many feel-good stories, the bad guy is only
bad because he has a backstory. So Scrooge is the way he is because
of a lonely childhood and relational failure. The Ghost of Christmas
Past shows how Scrooge became Scrooge-ish. To be sure, he made
bad decisions along the way, but the picture is of someone who was
fundamentally good until life got in the way. Obviously, the past is

not irrelevant. History matters, including our own histories. But my greatest danger is my own heart. Your biggest threat is not what can happen to you but what is going on inside of you. Bad thoughts and bad behavior cannot be explained solely by bad education, bad parents, or bad hurts in our past. We are all more sinful than sinned against. We enter the world with inherited guilt and a propensity for sin.

This is really important for how we conceive of lostness and missions. Those who never hear of Christ are *not* condemned because they do not believe in him. True, they are lost without this saving faith. But the lost are condemned because they are sinners. Your friends may ask, "What happens to the innocent tribesman who has never heard of Jesus? Won't he go to heaven?" Absolutely. But, of course, there are no innocent tribesmen. The wrath of God rests on those who do not believe in Christ because all of us are born into the world sinners with a sinful nature (John 3:36).

As important as it is to learn about unreached peoples and unengaged peoples, realize that these new terms are only helpful insofar as they highlight this biblical category of *lost* peoples. And lost doesn't mean they are backward people who need to be more like Westerners. Lost means spiritually dead, without God and without hope in the world, just like we all are apart from Christ. If we are going to help people—really help them with their deepest problem—we need to realize that without Christ we are not just sick or weak or ignorant. A life preserver will not do the trick. We are not drowning. We are not struggling. We are spiritually dead. The calling of missions is to call dead people back to life though the good news of Jesus Christ and the power of the Holy Spirit.

There was a movie when I was growing up called *Weekend at Bernie's*. I never saw it, and I'm sure it's not worth your time. The plot was pretty macabre: two guys find out their boss, Bernie, is dead, but in order to keep the mob from killing them, they have to convince everyone Bernie is alive and kicking. And so they bring him to parties and make him wave his hands around and all manner of silly business. The movie is a dark comedy where the living go to great lengths to make a dead person seem alive. Woe be unto us if our missions strategy amounts to the same thing: going into the world to help spiritually dead people look a little more alive.

What we are called to do is impossible in our own strength but entirely possible for God. Men, women, and children can be born again through the living and abiding Word of God (1 Pet. 1:23). And Peter says this word is the good news that was preached to you. Dead people come to life through words.

We cannot be saved apart from the work of the Spirit. And the work of the Spirit is never to be separated from the Word of God. The Word of God and the work of the Spirit are inextricably linked. And because of that, the work of the Spirit and the manifestation of Christ's glory are inextricably linked.

Now why is this important? In John 16, Jesus said the Spirit who comes will speak only what he hears. He will declare what he has been given. His mission is to glorify another (John 16:12–15). In other words, the Spirit acts as a spotlight to shine a brilliant light upon Christ so that people may see him, savor him, believe in him and live. The Spirit never works independently of making Christ known, which is why any notion of "anonymous Christians" is utterly mistaken and fundamentally anti-Trinitarian.

When I was in college, my world religion professor was a winsome, popular teacher. He was also very liberal and undermined a lot of the evangelical convictions of the students. I remember him saying, "Look, I believe in the sovereignty of God. And because God can do whatever he wants and the Spirit blows wherever he wills, I believe the Spirit of God can regenerate the hearts of Muslims and Buddhists and Hindus whether they know of Christ or not." The notion is quite popular among some evangelicals. It allows

Christians to affirm that only Christ saves, but then gives them the leeway of thinking that people can be saved without explicitly believing in Christ. So there may be people in other religions who don't know that they belong to Christ, and yet the Spirit has caused them to become born again and joined them to Christ, even though they've never heard of him and have never put their trust in him.

This view is called *inclusivism*, and some of you may hold to the view, not so much because it was taught to you, but because it seems good and feels good. In fact, even the great C. S. Lewis was mistaken on this account. He says in *Mere Christianity,* "There are people who do not accept the full Christian doctrine about Christ but who are so strongly attracted by him that they are his in a much deeper sense than they themselves understand. There are people in other religions who are being led by God's secret influence to concentrate on those parts of their religion which are in agreement with Christianity and who thus belong to Christ without knowing it."[16] You see the same idea in *The Chronicles of Narnia* where one of the worshippers of Tash is saved because it turns out he was really following Aslan without knowing it.[17]

There are many reasons why inclusivism does not work biblically, but one of the chief reasons has to do with the Trinity. To talk about the Spirit's work in the way my professor did, or even the way C. S. Lewis does in the passage above, is to fundamentally misunderstand the work of the Holy Spirit. The Spirit's work is always to reveal and glorify the Son. We cannot worship Christ apart from the work of the Spirit, and the Spirit does not want to be magnified except insofar as he points to Christ—which is why the symbolism of the early church was not the dove but the cross.

The Spirit works to throw a spotlight on the glory of Christ. The Spirit is not just working indiscriminately in sort of a secret "don't tell anybody, but wow, you're born again and you don't know it" kind of way. The Spirit longs to bring glory to a Christ who is known and revealed and seen and worshiped. Which is why we must go, and why we must speak. The doctrine of human inability—total depravity, the lostness of man, the sinfulness of sin, whatever you want to call it—is one of the great motivators for missions. There are billions of dead people in the world who need to hear the gospel of Jesus Christ and be born again to a living hope.

2. No One Can Come Unless the Father Draws (John 6:35–48, 60–65)

Jesus said to them, "I am the bread of life; whoever comes to me shall not hunger, and whoever believes in me shall never thirst. But I said to you that you have seen me and yet do not believe. All that the Father gives me will come to me, and whoever comes to me I will never cast out. For I have come down from heaven, not to do my own will but the will of him who sent me. And this is the will of him who sent me, that I should lose nothing of all that he has given me, but raise it up on the last day. For this is the will of my Father, that everyone who looks on the Son and believes in him should have eternal life, and I will raise him up on the last day." So the Jews grumbled about him, because he said, "I am the bread that came down from heaven." They said, "Is not this Jesus, the son of Joseph, whose father and mother we know? How does he now say, 'I have come down from heaven'?" Jesus answered them, "Do not grumble among yourselves. No one can come to me unless the Father who sent me draws him. And I will raise him up on the last day. It is written in the Prophets, 'And they will all be taught by God.' Everyone who has heard and learned from the Father comes to me—not that anyone has seen the Father except he who is from God; he has seen the Father. Truly, truly, I say to you, whoever believes has eternal life. I am the bread of life." (John 6:35–48)

And then picking up at verse 60, where Jesus finds the disciples perplexed by his statements that they must eat his flesh and drink his blood:

> When many of his disciples heard it, they said, "This is a hard saying; who can listen to it?" But Jesus, knowing in himself that his disciples were grumbling about this, said to them, "Do you take offense at this? Then what if you were to see the Son of Man ascending to where he was before? It is the Spirit who gives life; the flesh is no help at all. The words that I have spoken to you are spirit and life. But there are some of you who do not believe." (For Jesus knew from the beginning who those were who did not believe, and who it was who would betray him.) And he said, "This is why I told you that no one can come to me unless it is granted him by the Father." (John 6:60–65)

It would be hard for Jesus to articulate a higher view of divine sovereignty in salvation than he does in this passage.

- You see it in verse 37: "All that the Father gives me will come to me; whoever comes to me I will not cast out."
- In verse 44: "No one can come unless the Father who sent me draws him."
- And in verse 65: "This is why I told you no one can come unless it is granted to him by the Father."

If we pay attention to these staggering claims, they have the potential to change everything about our redemption. We see in these verses that the Father has a people chosen *for* Christ and chosen *in* Christ. We see that this number is fixed by divine determination—all that the Father gives will come to Christ, and none will come except those who are enabled to come. And we see that those who do come will in no way be cast out.

That last sentence, which is simply a restatement of verse 37, is absolutely crucial. Here's what I've heard before: "I can never believe this doctrine of election because it means that if I—or my sister, or grandmother, or my best friend, or whomever—come to Christ, in faith and sincerity, for grace and forgiveness, that Jesus could push me away because I'm not elect. There is no guarantee Christ will accept us. There can be no free offer of the gospel if election is true."

But of course such logic is patently not true, not according to Jesus' words in John 6. All who come to Christ come because God has drawn them. So if you come to Christ, he will never cast you away. A broken and contrite heart—gifts of his Spirit—he will not deny. The offer of the gospel is full and free, and because of God's electing and irresistible grace, it is possible for some to respond to this offer with faith and repentance. Human logic may say, "Why come if you may not have been chosen?" The Bible's logic says, "Come, because if you have been chosen by God, in time you will."

It is our confidence in the electing love of God and his irresistible grace that gives us any hope of success in preaching the gospel. We were dead in our sins and trespasses. We had no life, no hope, no ability for self-deliverance. And how were we saved? By the supernatural call of God. Maybe your parents told you, or a preacher told you, or you read it in a book, or you opened your Bible; but through whatever secondary means, the Spirit of God spoke to you through the word of God. He gave you a new heart. He caused you to be born again when you were completely dead. You weren't like Wesley from *The Princess Bride*—not just *mostly* dead, all dead.

Don't think that God only works miracles in people like you, with your skin color, or your background, or your education. Sinners are sinners everywhere, and God is the same everywhere. What he did for you, he can do for the unreached peoples of the world. God has elect from every nation, and his call is as irresistible in Africa and Asia as it is in America and Australia. Of course there are obstacles.

There are generational issues and language issues and cultural issues that can make for rocky soil. But a dead person is a dead person. It's a miracle to raise any of them. And God can do it. Anytime, anywhere, by the same gospel call through which you were saved. Why go to the nations unless you believe in this kind of God with this kind of sovereign power?

In John 5, Jesus says a time is coming when he will call forth the dead from their tombs, some to everlasting life and some to everlasting death (John 5:29). There is no uncertainty as to the efficacy of this call. Jesus will speak, and the dead will be raised. It's a good thing Jesus said, "*Lazarus,* come forth" (John 11:43), because if he had not prefaced the command with the name of his friend, all the tombs would have been emptied. Such is the power of the divine word.

You may say, "Why go share the gospel if God has chosen just some to believe?" The Bible's logic would have you ask, "Why go share the gospel *unless* God has chosen some to believe?" John Newton, the slave-trader-turned-pastor and hymn-writer once said, "If I were not a Calvinist, I think I should have no more hope of success in preaching to men than in preaching to horses and cows."[18]

As many as were appointed for eternal life believed. That's why we preach. That's why we share. That's why we go. And that line is not found in John Calvin or John Owen or John Piper, but in the Bible—Acts 13:48. God is the only one who can make light shine in our darkness. He's the only one who can give new life to the dead. He's the only one who can justify. He's the only one who can quicken the heart, the only one to renew the mind. Unless the Father draws, no one can come. We are born again, not of blood, nor of the will of the flesh, nor of the will of man, but of God (John 1:13). *Not by might, nor by power, but by my Spirit,* says the LORD (Zech. 4:6).

Belief in an electing, sovereign, all-powerful God does not discourage us from missions and evangelism. It is the only thing that gives us freedom and hope *in* missions and evangelism. You don't have to give them the hard sell. You don't have to be the infomercial ShamWow guy throwing in a free mop. The gospel is no limited-time offer. You don't have to put Jesus forward, "Now, with 50 percent more blessing!" You don't have to trick people or manipulate. You don't have to be afraid. You can be humble when you see results and hopeful when you see nothing at all. The doctrine of election gives us assurance that God *will* save, and the doctrine of irresistible grace gives us confidence that he *can* save. We will not go, we will not send, we will not suffer, without a firm conviction that our God is mighty to save and will not lose any of those appointed for eternal life.

I already mentioned Zechariah 4:6. Most Christians know and love that verse. But if you look ahead four more verses, you see what this divine power enable us to do. It doesn't mean we will walk on clouds and climb every mountain. It means we can press on through all the ordinary stuff of life, not despising the day of small things (Zech. 4:10). Zechariah 4 is about rebuilding the temple, which was going to take decades. It was going to take weeks and months and years of hard work with little to show for it. God wanted to remind his people that their labors would not be in vain. One day they would hold up the plumb line—the square, the level—and see the last brick in the last corner of the temple come into place. Do not despise the days and decades and lives of small things.

One of the best books I've read in recent years is *The Barbarian Conversion: From Paganism to Christianity* by Richard Fletcher. It's about the evangelization of Europe, which took the better part of a millennium. The point Fletcher emphasizes over and over is that the conversion and Christianization of Europe was very slow business. I don't know if the author is a Christian, but we can learn a lot from his historical assessment. He argues that Christianity eventually won over the West because of three factors: the demonstration of power, the faithful preaching, and dogged persistence. If we are ever going to make a difference for Christ—especially in the difficult work of the Great Commission—we have to become not just senders or goers, but stayers. And the only way we'll stay for the long haul is if we trust in the never failing, always timely providence of God.

That's what we see in Acts 18. Paul is facing opposition and wants to leave Corinth when Jesus appears to him in a dream, saying, "Do not be afraid, but go on speaking and do not be silent, for I am with you, and no one will attack you to harm you, for I have many in this city who are my people" (Acts 18:9–10). Without the doctrine of election, Paul wouldn't have pressed on in evangelism. You may say, "Well, that was nice for Paul. I'm glad he got a vision. But I'm not Paul, and I'm not in Corinth. Those promises aren't really for me." But in a very real way they are. Everything God promised to Paul he promises to you. His presence: I am with you (Matt. 28:20). His protection: not a hair can fall from your head apart from God willing it to be so (Matt. 10:29–30). And he promises you his providential oversight so that the word of God will not return empty (Isa. 55:10–11). He promises to every missionary and every evangelist that there will be people in heaven from every tribe and tongue and language and nation.

So if you go and labor among unreached peoples and labor for years with little or no visible fruit, you should remember the promise that there are some among that people group who are appointed for eternal life. That's how you can stay. That's how you can go. Samuel Zwemer, the Apostle to Islam, probably saw less than a dozen converts in his forty years as a missionary. God's sovereignty is our best fuel for ministry faithfulness.

God can motivate you to go from *here* to *there* in dozens of different ways. He gets you to see the plight of earthly suffering. He gets you to feel the peril of eternal suffering. We need to understand the great need that exists in the world. But in addition to peril and plight, we need lots of promises—promises so you'll go, promises so you'll stay, promises so you'll last. What I've learned from our missionaries is that serving overseas is less glamorous and more mundane than most people think. It's like living a normal life, except less convenient and farther from your family. What will keep you there? A steady faith in God's sovereignty gives you the confidence to stick around, trusting the word of God is more than enough to do the work of God.

3. The Sheep Hear the Shepherd's Voice
(John 10:7–15, 27–30)

> So Jesus again said to them, "Truly, truly, I say to you, I am the door of the sheep. All who came before me are thieves and robbers, but the sheep did not listen to them. I am the door. If anyone enters by me, he will be saved and will go in and out and find pasture. The thief comes only to steal and kill and destroy. I came that they may have life and have it abundantly. I am the good shepherd. The good shepherd lays down his life for the sheep. He who is a hired hand and not a shepherd, who does not own the sheep, sees the wolf coming and leaves the sheep and flees, and the wolf snatches them and scatters them. He flees because he is a hired hand and cares nothing for the sheep. I am the good shepherd. I know my own and my own know me, just as the Father knows me and I know the Father; and I lay down my life for the sheep. . . .
>
> "My sheep hear my voice, and I know them, and they follow me. I give them eternal life, and they will never perish, and no one will snatch them out of my hand. My Father, who has given them to me, is greater than all, and no one is able to snatch them out of the Father's hand. I and the Father are one." (John 10:7–15, 27–30)

Jesus is a *good* shepherd. Isn't that good news? In the Vulgate, the old Latin translation, Jesus says in verse 14, *"ego sum pastor bonus."* The word *bonus* here means good, not extra special or additional. But knowing the Latin can help us remember that as much as we love our earthly pastors, we have a bonus pastor in heaven, a good shepherd. Jesus is the Good Shepherd; he's our best shepherd. He knows the sheep. He cares for the sheep. He didn't pursue a career in messiahship because carpentry was difficult. He's not just trying to make a living. He's not a hired hand. He laid down his life because that's how good a shepherd he is.

I read a story one time about a family in the Florida Everglades. The family was in the backyard playing when the husband and wife saw an alligator come out of the bush, grab their small child, and head back toward the water. The parents were understandably horrified. The husband began immediately looking for a weapon—a stone, a bat, a gun, something he could use to attack the gator. But while he was looking for the right tool, the mother launched into a dead sprint. She ran full speed toward the alligator, jumped on his back and started kicking, hitting, biting, and screaming. The alligator, probably more disoriented than hurt, let go of the child and slinked back into the water. The mom grabbed the child and ran for safety. Then she fainted. She was no hired hand. She was the momma, and nobody messes with momma bear's little cub. She was like a good shepherd laying down her life for the sheep.

And I want you to notice that Jesus' death is explicitly for the sheep—not the wolves, not the goats, not the pigs, but for the ones who hear his voice and come. This doctrine is sometimes called "limited atonement," meaning the atoning death of Christ was limited to the elect. *Limited*, however, is not the best term. It makes it sound like we have some interest constricting the power or God or narrowing the love of God. It would be better to say the death of Christ purchased a *particular redemption*. In one sense, it's certainly true that

Jesus died for everyone, if you mean that his death was sufficient for all or that Christ's death should be proclaimed to all. But Jesus did not die a substitutionary atoning death for every individual who would ever live. If that were the case, then everyone's sins would be forgiven, and we would be left with an unbiblical universalism. Scripture tells us that Christ's death was intended to be for his sheep and savingly effective only for them.

That's why in John 6, Jesus says he came to save those the Father had given to him.

And why Matthew 1:21 says Jesus will save "his people from their sins."

And why John 15:13 says he laid down his life for his friends.

And why Acts 20:28 says Christ died for the church.

And why Ephesians 5:25 says he gave his life for his bride.

Christ's death was, by divine design, an atoning sacrifice for the sins of those who by election already died and, by faith, would belong to God. The atonement is limited in the sense that the redemption is particularly for those upon whom God set his affections from eternity past. The doctrine reminds us that we are God's treasured possession and that he loves his own in a way that is utterly unique. Do you fully grasp what it means that God loves you in Christ? I saw a T-shirt one time that said, "Smile Jesus Loves You." And underneath this head-line were the words, "But Then Again He Loves Everybody." We sometimes imagine God's love to be like this: "He loves everyone. I'm a part of the 'everyone,' so I guess he loves me too." But that's not how the Bible describes the love of God. His love for you—if you are a believer—is a specific, unique, particular, effective, redeeming, electing love. That's good news.

The stunning implication of John 10 (and dozens of other pas-sages) is that Christ didn't die to make a way for you to be saved; he died in your place to save you. Do you see the difference? The view that says Christ's death only made us save-able is the view that actually limits the atonement. Christ died so that he might infallibly secure our salvation. As Charles Spurgeon put it, "Through Christ's death [we] not only may be saved, but are saved, must be saved and cannot by any possibility run the hazard of being anything but saved."[19] That's the better news and the bigger glory of particular redemption.

If the atonement is not particularly and only for the sheep, then either we have universalism (Christ died in everyone's place) or we have something less than full substitutionary atonement. For universal atonement to be true, Christ must not have died in our place so that we died in his death and live through his resurrection. Instead, he must have died to make a way for people to believe and be saved. The question is this: Did Jesus die to remove the final obstacle for our salvation, or did he die so that in his death we would have salvation?

Note these powerful words from J. I. Packer:

It cannot be over emphasized that we have not seen the full meaning of the cross until we have seen it as the center of the gospel. Flanked on the one hand by total inability and unconditional election and on the other by irresistible grace and final preservation. For the full meaning of the cross only appears when the atonement is defined in terms of these four truths. Christ died to save a certain company of helpless sinners upon whom God has set his free saving love. Christ's death insured the calling and keeping of all whose sins he bore. That is what Calvary means and what it meant. The cross saved, the cross saves.[20]

I belabor this point, not to belittle anyone who holds to a different theology, but to give Jesus Christ his full glory as one who fully saves. The Son of God doesn't come to us saying, "Well, I've done my part. I've laid down my life. Now, if you would just accept me and ask me into your heart." There used to be an old evangelistic tract set up like an election ballot. The ballot had Jesus voting for heaven, the devil voting for hell, and a blank spot for you to break the tie. That's not the gospel. The New Testament gives us a choice to make, but it is not a choice to break some cosmic tie between God and Satan. Our God is not that small!

With this doctrine of particular redemption, we can go and can tell people that in Christ, through faith, God not only made a way for his people to be saved, but he saved his people to the uttermost. Christ was pierced for our transgressions. He was crushed for our iniquities (Isa. 53:5). He purchased with his blood people for God from every tribe and language and people and nation (Rev. 5:9). He bore our sins in his body on the tree so that we might infallibly die to sin and assuredly live for righteousness, for his wounds did not merely make healing available, they healed us (1 Pet. 2:24).

God Preserves His Saints

All of this theology leads naturally, biblically, and joyfully to the last of the so-called Five Points: the perseverance, or preservation, of the saints. Jesus says in John 10:28, "I give them eternal life, and they will never perish, and no one will snatch them out of my hand." Those who belong to Christ are promised eternal life because in a real way they have already been given eternal life. When we are joined to Christ in faith we are made participants in his triumphant, never-failing, never-faltering, eternal life. While our sense of communion with Christ may ebb and flow, our union with Christ is fixed and firm.

This is far different from easy-believism. The doctrine of the perseverance of the saints is no excuse for the cheap grace of decisionistic Christianity. You know: raise your hand, walk the aisle, sign a card, throw your pinecone into the fire, make a one-time decision, and then enjoy eternal fire insurance the rest of your life, no matter how you live. The Bible has no place for a Christianity without repentance, without obedience, without fighting the good fight, without running the race to completion. At the same time, we see from Jesus—and from Romans 8 and from 1 John and from Jude— that truly regenerate, born-again, justified, grace-filled disciples cannot alternately fall away. In one sense, we come into possession of eternal life when we believe, and eternal life can never be temporary.

There is no security like gospel security. All over the world, all the time, we hear geopolitical security issues. People talk about food security and the need to increase crop yields. People talk about water security and the need for new wells and drinkable water. People talk about national security and wars and rumors of war. No matter how wise you are, no matter how talented your group of volunteers, no matter how accomplished your NGO, you will not be able to fix any of these problems with ultimate, lasting security.

But you can go, and you can promise, in the name of Jesus, eternal security. You can tell the nations that there is one, and only one, who can save, one who can keep, one who can forgive your sins and give you life that never ends.

Know, Go, and Stay

We have a big God. That's what this chapter has been about. I'm not interested in affixing labels or signing you up for the right club. I am very interested in seeing God get all his glory and getting his people to the ends of the earth. We can risk everything because God risks nothing. We can be willing to be surprised because God is never surprised. We can give up our security because in Christ we have all the security we really need.

The purpose of all of this theology is not only for us to *know*, but that we might *go*. If you are going to tell others about Jesus, you need to know who this Jesus is. You need to know what he has accomplished. You need to know for whom he died. You need to know what sort of promises he has made and what sort of promises you get to proclaim. You need to know that if you give your life for the hope of the nations, and if your parents don't understand, and if your friends think you're nuts, and if you have to sleep with mosquito nets or ride a mini-bus two hours a day, that your labors will not be in vain.

This glorious Big-God theology tells us what to say and provides the best reasons for going out there to say it. Why give everything you have for a message that is not necessary, a plan that is not fixed, a cross that does not save, a grace that cannot conquer, and a promise that may not hold?

Oh the deep, deep love of Jesus! Praise God for the robust glorious gospel of the Lord Jesus Christ with all of its particularity and all of its angles and all of its doctrinal comprehensiveness. This is a message worth living for and a message worth dying for. The peoples of the earth need to hear it, and those whom God has chosen, and for whom Christ savingly died, will irresistibly believe it, receive it, and live forever. That's why we send. That's why we go. That's why we stay.

CHAPTER 4

The Death of Death
in the Death of Christ

━━━━ Conrad Mbewe ━━━━

The goal of missions is to establish the kingdom of God. The kingdom of God is that sphere where the true God of heaven is adored, loved, served, and obeyed from joyful hearts that relish the God they have come to know.

How is this kingdom established here on earth? It is not through the barrel of the gun, or the decrees of earthly potentates, but through the proclamation of a message. In this chapter, we will take a look at the message that we are to go with into this world in order to establish God's kingdom in the hearts of men and women.

Though the entire Bible is full of this message, in Romans 3 we find in capsule form the good news we are to bring to a world that is lost in sin and under the wrath of God. It is the news of a full and free righteousness that is introduced in this epistle with the words "but now" found at the beginning of Romans 3:21.

The apostle Paul paints a bleak picture concerning the world under the wrath of God from Romans 1:18 all the way to 3:20. He gives the backdrop so that when he brings in the good news, his readers will appreciate that this is the best news in the universe. Thus he shows that the nations are under God's wrath, and God's old-covenant people, the Jews, also are under God's wrath because they too are sinners. Any effort on the part of the Jews to put on some semblance of righteousness is like trying to pull your leg out of quicksand and causing the other leg to sink twice deeper. It is completely useless. Paul captures this helpless and hopeless situation in the words, "There is no distinction: for all have sinned and fall short of the glory of God" (Rom. 3:22–23).

When Paul brings both Gentiles and Jews to see the pitch-black darkness of their helplessness and hopelessness under the judgment of God, he then turns on the bright light of the gospel for them to see their only hope. He calls this hope "justification," and he says it comes to them "by his grace as a gift, through the redemption that is in Christ Jesus" (Rom. 3:24). His point is that it is not something that you earn or "merit." It is something that God freely gives. It is given freely to people who, in fact, deserve the opposite. Surely, that must be good news! If you know that you have offended a righteous God and deserve his wrath, then it must be a free gift when God pardons you.

The apostle Paul goes into a little more detail concerning this redemption when he writes that it is in him "whom God put forward as a propitiation by his blood, to be received by faith" (Rom. 3:25). This is a pregnant statement. And it is this statement that I would like us to think about in greater detail in this chapter, because it contains our message to the world. In it, we have the heart of the good news. It is the good news of a bloody cross.

The Bad News

In order to appreciate this good news, we must begin with the bad news, which is best summarized in one word: *death*. This is evident from the warning that God gave to Adam at the dawn of history. "The LORD God commanded the man, saying, 'You may surely eat of every tree of the garden, but of the tree of the knowledge of good and evil you shall not eat, for in the day that you eat of it you shall surely die'" (Gen. 2:16–17). And that is precisely what happened. Adam and Eve died.

The first form of death that occurred upon Adam and Eve eating the forbidden fruit was *spiritual death*. Corruption entered into their beings. Thus when God came to meet with them in the cool of the evening, Adam and Eve scampered for cover. They ran away from the very God with whom they once used to meet in fellowship, affection, and holy adoration. This spiritual death also led to a breakdown in the relationship between Adam and Eve. When God confronted Adam about what he had done, in Genesis 3:12, his answer amounts to saying, "It is this woman whom you dumped here with me; she is the cause of all my problems." Does that sound familiar? There is nothing new under the sun! This spiritual death did not end between Adam and Eve. When they gave birth to children, it was passed on to them. Hence, it is not long before we find their eldest son, Cain, murdering his brother, Abel, out of envy. Surely, something had gone wrong spiritually. It was spiritual death. The fellowship and connectivity that had been there with God was now gone.

The second form of death that occurred upon Adam and Eve eating the forbidden fruit was *physical death*. We have already noted this from the death of Abel at the hands of his brother Cain. The reality of physical death is emphasized in Genesis 5 when the author ends the short biographical sketches of every individual (except Enoch) with the words, ". . . and he died" (vv. 5, 8, 11, 14, 17, 20, 27, and 31). That is human history summarized for us over and over. Every day, every hour, every minute, and indeed every second, someone somewhere breathes his last and dies. Scientists tell us that we are, in fact, born already dying. The seed of decay and death is already in us from conception.

The third form of death—which is the worst—is an *eternal death*. The Bible refers to it as the second death. "As for the cowardly, the faithless, the detestable, as for murderers, the sexually immoral, sorcerers, idolaters, and all liars, their portion will be in the lake that burns with fire and sulfur, which is the second death" (Rev. 21:8). This is an eternal death. It is when God finally sends the sinner to that place of utter darkness, where there is weeping and gnashing of teeth. It is a place of fire and torment, where "the worm does not die." The uncompromisingly righteous God must eternally punish sinners.

So, if there is one word that describes our misery as a human race, it is the word "death." It hangs like a dark cloud over our heads, threatening a storm from which we will never recover, serving as our great common denominator of fear (Heb. 2:15). Our greatest tragedy, therefore, is not a lack of money or poor health facilities. It is death!

The Good News

The good news that we take to the world is that this same God, whose judgment is death, has provided an answer to this tragedy through the person of his Son, Jesus Christ. Death has died in the death of Christ. That is what Paul meant when he said, "[We] are justified by his grace as a gift, through the redemption that is in Christ Jesus" (Rom. 3:24).

To redeem means to buy back. It suggests that there has been a loss due to a liability. You cannot have that which your heart longs for until a payment has been made. Perhaps it is a loan that you have received from the bank upon depositing your title deeds with the banker. You cannot have your title deed back until you have paid back that loan in full. That is precisely the human condition. We are held in bondage to sin and death until a payment is made on our behalf to God the lawgiver. The apostle Paul says here that Jesus Christ has made this payment.

When we think of the coming of the Lord Jesus Christ into this world to redeem us from death, we must see his work of redemption under three important categories.

Suffering

Jesus is God. He is the second person of the blessed, holy Trinity, through whom the whole of creation came into existence. In eternity, he entered into a covenant with his Father. Theologians refer to it as the Covenant of Redemption. In that covenant, his task was to come to earth and suffer for the sins of his people. Thus, the Son of God came into this world "clothed in human nature"—fully God and fully man—to fulfill this assignment. He was hunted like a wild animal from the crib to the cross. He knew suffering throughout his life. In Gethsemane, he fell on his knees and pleaded with the Father because he knew he was about to drink the full cup of God's wrath. His soul was about to undergo immense and intense suffering. Hence, he prayed, "My Father, if it be possible, let this cup pass from me; nevertheless, not as I will, but as you will" (Matt. 26:39). He prayed until his sweat became like great drops of blood falling to the ground. God the Father sent an angel to strengthen him for the last mile of the journey. He was finally captured, taken through a mock trial, and crucified. It is important to note that he freely handed himself over to his captors. He truly suffered.

Substitution

On the cross, Jesus did not only suffer physically. He experienced the wrath of God that his people ought to have experienced because of their sin. The Holy Spirit helped him as he drank in our hell on our behalf, as our substitute. To the cry, "My God, my God, why have you forsaken me?" God's answer would have been, "It is because you are standing in the place of those whom I have given to you. You must make full payment for their sin." As the apostle Paul explained to the Corinthians, "For our sake he made him to be sin who knew no sin, so that in him we might become the righteousness of God" (2 Cor. 5:21). Jesus was a substitute. We deserved to die. There was absolutely nothing we could do to turn that around. We had messed up. The God of justice was to bring his sword of justice upon us, but Jesus intervened. He took our place, and the sword came upon him. That is the only way you can explain Calvary.

Satisfaction

Jesus Christ rose from the dead, showing that God was satisfied with the payment that was made for our sin. I will explain this truth at greater length than the first two because it is the height of the good news. Faith needs to grasp this. It is in order to make this truth plain that the apostle Paul in Romans 3:25 uses a word that we do not often hear today. It is the word "propitiation." He writes that Jesus is the one "whom God put forward as a propitiation by his blood, to be received by faith."

To a Jew who was familiar with Greek, this word pointed to the mercy seat in the Temple where the high priest would go into the Holy of Holies once a year with the blood of a slain animal. He would pour the blood on the mercy seat. His message would be, "Yes, Lord, we deserved to die. You are a holy and just God. Sin deserves death. But because of your mercy, you have provided that another should take our place and die our death. Another has taken our place. Here is the evidence: the shed blood. Be appeased. Become propitious toward us. May your justice be satisfied."

The Apostle took that picture and brought its light to bear upon Calvary. He said that God set forth Jesus in exactly the same way that the high priest set forth the sacrifice of atonement. This time it is his own blood that is shed. Jesus is both the high priest and the sacrifice. Just as the animal would suffer as a substitute to satisfy the wrath of God, so also Jesus suffered as a substitute on behalf of his people to satisfy the wrath of God against their sin. Just as the high priest would come out of the Holy of Holies alive and announce the "Shalom" (peace) to the people, so also Jesus rose from the dead and speaks peace to those who trust in him.

This is the good news that we share with the world. When we look at the cross and see the mangled form of the Son of God as though he had been attacked by some ferocious beast in the jungles of Africa, we say, "There go I but for the grace of God." When we hear him cry, "It is finished," we jump up and shout, "Hallelujah! Our sins have been fully paid for by another, the Lord Jesus Christ." Our death has died in the person of God's own Son. He offered himself as an atoning sacrifice. He suffered the wrath of God that ought to have sunk us deeper than the grave into the flames of hell. He has reconciled us to God. And in reconciling us to God, Jesus secured our justification, sanctification, and adoption, all the way to our glorification. So, the author of the letter to the Hebrews could write, "In bringing many sons to glory, it was fitting that God, for whom and through whom everything exists, should make the author of their salvation perfect through suffering" (Heb. 2:10 NIV 1984).

It is important for us to see that Jesus did not only make it possible for us to be reconciled to God. He effected this reconciliation. Our death died on Calvary; it did not faint! Thus we can sing,

My sin—O the bliss of this glorious thought—
My sin—not in part but the whole—

Is nailed to his cross and I bear it no more
Praise the Lord! Praise the Lord! O my soul!

Proof That God Is Satisfied

On the annual Day of Atonement in the Old Testament, the proof that God had accepted the sacrifice was that the high priest came out of the Holy of Holies alive. With respect to the saving work of Christ, there are two phases that prove that God had accepted his sacrifice.

The first phase is the resurrection. Jesus often spoke about both his death and resurrection. The two went together. After his resurrection, he reminded his disciples, "Thus it is written, that the Christ should suffer and on the third day rise from the dead" (Luke 24:46). To John, the last surviving apostle some decades later, Jesus says, "Fear not, I am the first and the last, and the living one. I died, and behold I am alive forevermore, and I have the keys of Death and Hades" (Rev. 1:17–18). He has vanquished death. As glorious as the death of Christ on the cross might be, it is absolutely essential that the story not end there. He rose again from the dead, nevermore to die.

The members of the Sanhedrin were fearful of this matter. So, they asked that a squad of well-trained soldiers should guard Jesus' tomb.

The next day, that is, after the day of Preparation, the chief priests and the Pharisees gathered before Pilate and said, "Sir, we remember how that impostor said, while he was still alive, 'After three days I will rise.' Therefore order the tomb to be made secure until the third day, lest his disciples go and steal him away and tell the people, 'He has risen from the dead,' and the last fraud will be worse than the first." Pilate said to them, "You have a guard of soldiers. Go, make it as secure as you can."

So they went and made the tomb secure by sealing the stone and setting a guard. (Matt. 27:62–66)

The body was not there three days later. They had to find a way to explain it. The soldiers were told to lie, but surely their story must have been unconvincing. On one hand, this was a squad of well-trained soldiers. How could a bunch of untrained and unsophisticated fishermen and tax collectors steal a dead body from them? On the other hand, if they were truly sleeping, then how did they know that the disciples had stolen the body? It does not square. Something extraordinary happened. To borrow the words of the hymn-writer,

Death cannot keep its prey, Jesus my Saviour;
He tore the bars away, Jesus my Lord!
Up from the grave he arose;
With a mighty triumph o'er his foes;
He arose a victor from the dark domain,
And he lives forever, with his saints to reign.
He arose! He arose! Hallelujah! Christ arose!

Instead of coming up with the lamest of excuses, we should all heed the counsel of yet another hymn-writer who says,

Crown Him the Lord of life, who triumphed over the grave,
And rose victorious in the strife for those He came to save.
His glories now we sing, who died, and rose on high,
Who died eternal life to bring, and lives that death may die.

The second phase is that Jesus entered heaven itself as our advocate with the Father. The writer of the letter to the Hebrews says, "When Christ appeared as a high priest of the good things that have come, then through the greater and more perfect tent (not made with hands, that is, not of this creation) he entered once for all into the holy places, not by means of the blood of goats and calves but by means of his own blood, thus securing an eternal redemption" (Heb. 9:11–12).

Unlike the earthly priests who offered the blood of bulls and goats in an equally earthly temple, Jesus entered heaven itself with his own blood to appear before God on our behalf. He has gone ahead of us into the place where eternal decisions are made that assign to us our eternal destinies. Jesus Christ the righteous one has gone there to speak to God on our behalf. Thus, by the power of his intercessory work in heaven, based squarely on his death on the cross, all those for whom he died will be given grace sufficient to bring them to heaven. This is good news. It is the news we take to the world.

Our Appropriate Response

Our first response to this good news is that we must believe. Its benefits are not given to you automatically. You must repent and believe the good news. The most famous verse in the Bible says, "God so loved the world, that he gave his only Son, that whoever believes in him should not perish but have eternal life" (John 3:16). The death that has brought misery upon the human race has been quenched in the person of God's own Son. Eternal life is yours for the receiving. Believe it! It is only when you believe it that you can look death defiantly in the face and say, "O death, where is your victory? O death, where is your sting?" (1 Cor. 15:55).

Our second response is that of worship. We worship God because this salvation has opened our eyes to who God is. We sense something of his excellent beauty in creation, in providence, and especially in our salvation. Thus we adore him. This is especially the case because of our sense of indebtedness to God. He has saved us freely by his grace. Thus, with the apostle Paul we shout in exultation, "'Who has ever given to God, that God should repay him?' For from him and through him and to him are all things. To him be the glory forever!" (Rom. 11:35–36 NIV). Nothing inspires worship more than an appreciation of God's grace in salvation.

Our final response is that of sharing this good news in evangelistic and missionary enterprise. You cannot believe this good news and then keep it to yourself. That is impossible. As the apostle Paul would put it, "Christ's love compels us" (2 Cor. 5:14 NIV 1984). This is the kind of news that you want the whole world to know.

Does this message of divine love burn within you? Then go and share the message with those who are held bound by their fear of death, and who are tumbling down into the grave. Stand in their way and shout, "Death has died in the death of Christ." Cross the oceans and the continents and speak not only of a God of holiness and justice, but also a God of mercy and love and grace.

CHAPTER 5

Seeing Jesus Properly

The Lord to Gladly Obey Forever

— Richard Chin —

Seeing Jesus properly is a matter of life and death. To see Jesus revealed in Scripture is gloriously breathtaking and can only compel us to gladly obey him forever. But according to Jesus, to see him otherwise can align yourself with Satan!

How do you *see* Jesus? Everybody sees Jesus one way or another. Every religion does.[21] Every social commentator does. Even off-beat bands do.[22]

But how do *you* see Jesus?

Just imagine you've come home from a wedding. And you get a little bored. So you log onto Facebook and discover that a friend has uploaded a number of photos from that very wedding. As you look through them—be honest—who are you really looking for? Yourself!

In the next few pages, I want to show you a few Facebook photos from chapter 8 of the Gospel according to Mark. And I want to ask if you can picture yourself in any of them. For each of these photos depicts a different way of *seeing* Jesus that has eternal consequences.

Photograph 1: Seeing Jesus like the Pharisees

In Jesus' days on earth, the Pharisees were a movement of lay-men. They were not priests. But they were still *very* religious. They wanted to preserve their religious traditions just as much as preserving God's Law. This is one of the major reasons they oppose Jesus here in Mark 8.

> The Pharisees came and began to argue with him, seeking from him a sign from heaven to test him. And he sighed deeply in his spirit and said, "Why does this generation seek a sign? Truly, I say to you, no sign will be given to this generation." And he left them, got into the boat again, and went to the other side." (Mark 8:11–13)

The Pharisees *saw* Jesus as someone who would destroy their religious traditions.

So they were never really interested in his answers. They just wanted to *test* him.

Could you possibly be in this photo?

Perhaps you are reading this book because you are seriously considering becoming a missionary. But it just *may* be that you come from a religious tradition that Jesus challenges.

He says, for example, that he did not come "to call the righteous, but sinners" (Matt. 9:13). He came "to seek and to save the lost" (Luke 19:10). As you read the rest of the New Testament, it becomes overwhelmingly clear that we *cannot contribute anything of merit to our salvation*. We are all lost sinners deserving his judgment. The only thing we can contribute to our salvation is our sin! We can only trust what he alone has done to save us.

Does this challenge any of the traditions you have grown up with?

If so, there's just a slim possibility that you see Jesus like the Pharisees.

When they saw Jesus confronting and overturning their traditions, they sought to test him by asking for a sign. But did you note Jesus' response? He "sighed deeply in his spirit" (v. 12). He groaned! And in response "he left them" (v. 13).

Isn't that a chilling thought? The Lord of the Universe *left them*! Seeing Jesus properly really is a matter of life and death.

Photograph 2: Seeing Jesus like the Disciples

As the narrative continues, the disciples leave the Pharisees and get into a boat with Jesus. But look what happens:

> Now they had forgotten to bring bread, and they had only one loaf with them in the boat. And he cautioned them, saying, "Watch out; beware of the leaven of the Pharisees and the leaven of Herod." (Mark 8:14–15)

What is Jesus talking about? Perhaps reflect on it for just thirty seconds before reading on.

When Jesus speaks of *leaven*, he is referring to yeast which mixes through the whole batch of dough when making bread. And here he is either referring to the *teaching* of the Pharisees and Herod, or to these people *themselves* who stand opposed to Jesus. So, he says, watch out for their opposition.

But the disciples *understandably* think that Jesus was talking about bread, because leaven (yeast) is used to make bread, and they had neglected to bring along enough to feed themselves. But look at Jesus' reply:

And they began discussing with one another the fact that they had no bread. And Jesus, aware of this, said to them, "Why are you discussing the fact that you have no bread? Do you not yet perceive or understand? Are your hearts hardened? Having eyes do you not see, and having ears do you not hear? And do you not remember? When I broke the five loaves for the five thousand, how many baskets full of broken pieces did you take up?" They said to him, "Twelve." "And the seven for the four thousand, how many baskets full of broken pieces did you take up?" And they said to him, "Seven." And he said to them, "Do you not yet understand?" (Mark 8:16–21)

Jesus is basically saying, "You disciples have already seen me feed crowds of thousands of people recently (in desolate places) just like God fed Israel in a desolate place after the exodus from Egypt (see Mark 6:30–44 and 8:1–10). And there were *basketfuls* of bread left over! Don't you think I could feed you now? So if I did the same miracle with the one loaf you have now, there would be enough bread left over to sink this boat! So why are you arguing about not having enough bread?"

As far as Jesus is concerned, they were still nonbelievers, even though they had given up everything to follow him. Why? Their hearts were hardened because they still didn't see Jesus properly. They still did not see Jesus as their divine provider.

Could you be in this photo?

Perhaps you too claim to be a follower of Jesus, and yet you still find it hard to believe that Jesus can do what God does. Are there times when you've asked Jesus to do something—like fix a broken relationship, or heal a sickness, or get you through a time of trial—only to discover that he doesn't appear to be answering? Perhaps Jesus still feels distant to you and your prayers appear so hollow. And you're left wondering whether you really believe that he is willing and able to answer you. Are you tempted to give up on him?

I have two dear friends who were engaged in full-time Christian ministry, but sadly over the years became disillusioned with Jesus because of trials they could not endure. Now they live as unbelievers. Their hearts have been hardened.

Could *you* possibly be in this photo? There's no point entertaining the thought of becoming a missionary if your heart is not going in the right direction toward Jesus. Seeing Jesus properly really is a matter of life and death.

Photograph 3: Seeing Jesus like the Ordinary People of the Land

And Jesus went on with his disciples to the villages of Caesarea Philippi. And on the way he asked his disciples, "Who do people say that I am?" And they told him, "John the Baptist; and others say, Elijah; and others, one of the prophets." (Mark 8:27–28)

Some people saw Jesus as one of the great prophets.

Concerning John, Jesus said, "Among those born of women there has arisen no one greater than John the Baptist" (Matt. 11:11). Assuming no one is born of a man, Jesus is saying that John is the greatest human being ever to have been born up till that time! And some of the ordinary people of the land think that Jesus is not just *like* John, but that he *is* John come back from the dead. Remember, John had already been beheaded (Mark 6:14–29).

Still others saw Jesus as the great Elijah come back from the dead. Elijah was one of the great prophets of the Old Testament. In fact, he never died but was taken up into heaven in a fiery chariot (2 Kings 2).

Could you possibly be in this photo? Could you possibly become a missionary yet still not see Jesus properly?

John Wesley did. He became a missionary to Georgia. Yet listen to his words: "My chief motive is to save my own soul. . . . I hope to learn the true sense of the Gospel of Jesus Christ by preaching it to the heathen." When he reached Georgia, he was asked, "Do you know Jesus Christ?" And he answered, "I know he is the Saviour of the world." But when asked, "Do you know if he has saved you?" Wesley replied, "I hope he has died to save me."[23]

Like the ordinary people of the land, Wesley had a positive view of Jesus. He was so positive that he became a missionary. And yet he did not see him properly. Yes, Jesus is the Savior of the World, but he is more, much more. And Wesley only discovered that *after* his missionary service.

Sincerity does not equal truth. To see Jesus *sincerely* is not the same as seeing Jesus *properly*.

Seeing Jesus properly really is a matter of life and death.

Seeing Jesus Properly

In the middle of Mark 8, there is an odd two-staged miracle that Jesus performs.

And they came to Bethsaida. And some people brought to him a blind man and begged him to touch him. And he took the blind man by the hand and led him out of the village, and when he had spit on his eyes and laid his hands on him, he asked him, "Do you see anything?" And he looked up and said, "I see people, but they look like trees, walking." Then Jesus laid his hands on his eyes again; and he opened his eyes, his sight was restored, and he saw everything clearly. And he sent him to his home, saying, "Do not even enter the village." (Mark 8:22–26)

Why is this account placed right in the middle of the other incidents in Mark 8? And why does Jesus need two attempts to heal the blind man? Was Jesus tired that night? Was he off his healing game?

No, this story is placed here to show that unless you see Jesus properly, your eyes are not fully opened.

It is an illustration. Isn't that exactly what happened to Peter? At first, Peter *seems* to see Jesus properly. When Jesus asks him, "Who do you say that I am?" Peter answers, "You are the Christ" (v. 29).

He saw Jesus as the one God promised all along, the Messiah who would rule the world with all power and authority—King of kings and Lord of lords. And he was right about that. This is the turning point in Mark's gospel where finally one of the disciples appears to see Jesus as he really is.

It is one of the greatest moments in history. But look what happens next:

And he began to teach them that the Son of Man must suffer many things and be rejected by the elders and the chief priests and the scribes and be killed, and after three days rise again. And he said this plainly. And Peter took him aside and began to rebuke him. But turning and seeing his disciples, he rebuked Peter and said, "Get behind me, Satan! For you are not setting your mind on the things of God, but on the things of man." (Mark 8:31–33)

Alongside one of history's greatest moments is one of history's greatest blunders. Peter tries to rebuke the Lord of lords! Effectively he says, "Jesus, you are the Messiah who will rule over all, but let me tell you how to rule."

And Jesus sees Peter's rebuke as coming from the very flames of hell. For Peter *not* to see Jesus properly was to align himself with Satan.

So here is the lesson of the two-staged miracle in verses 22–26: Our eyes can be opened to see who Jesus is, but until you see him as the "Son of Man" who must suffer, die, and rise again, your eyes are not fully opened. You do not see Jesus properly. And you will not see the radical implications for your life.

See Him as the "Son of Man"

Throughout the Gospels, Jesus most often refers to himself *in the third person* as the "Son of Man." It is his favorite title by far. And it comes from the pages of Daniel, chapter 7, where the prophet Daniel has a nightmare about four terrible beasts coming *out of the sea*.

In his nightmare, the first beast is like a lion, and it has the wings of an eagle. The second beast looks like a bear with three ribs of another carcass. The third beast looks like a leopard with four wings on its back. The fourth beast is *not* like the first three. It's terrifyingly indescribable with large iron teeth that crush its victims.

And we learn that these beasts represent *terrifying* kingdoms that ruled the world of their day. In Daniel's day, the Babylonian kingdom ruled and destroyed Jerusalem. Then the Kingdom of the Medes and Persians ruled, after which the Kingdom of Greece ruled (especially under Alexander the Great). Then the Roman kingdom came. All of them were terrifying and formidable in their day. We're not sure which kingdoms the beasts referred to *exactly*.

But the main point of Daniel 7 is that although these human kingdoms will be terrifying, they will be transient. Why? Because God is in absolute control.

In the middle of Daniel's nightmare concerning the terrifying beasts, there is a vision that makes him look up. And look what he sees:

As I looked, thrones were placed, and the Ancient of Days took his seat; his clothing was white as snow, and the hair of his head like pure wool; his throne was fiery flames; its wheels were burning fire. A stream of fire issued and came out from before him; a thousand thousands served him, and ten thousand times ten thousand stood before him; the court sat in judgment, and the books were opened. (Dan. 7:9–10)

Here is a picture of God, described as the "Ancient of Days." Here is the eternal one who is in absolute control, seated on his throne, with thousands and thousands of servants attending him. No matter how terrifying any kingdom is, God not only created them, but he also judges them. Nothing is out of his control. Nothing is beyond his justice. Nothing can thwart his plans.

And central to his plan is the "Son of Man."

I saw in the night visions, and behold, with the clouds of heaven there came one *like a son of man,* and he came to the Ancient of Days and was presented before him. And to him was given dominion and glory and a kingdom, that all peoples, nations, and languages should serve him; his dominion is an everlasting dominion, which shall not pass away, and his kingdom one that shall not be destroyed. (Dan. 7:13–14)

Human kingdoms may be formidable and terrifying like the Roman kingdom, or Nazi Germany, or terrorist organizations like Al-Qaeda, Al-Shabaab, or the Taliban. But they will be transient! They will be brought to justice! And the Son of Man will rule over them forever.

Please note that the Son of Man is *not* beast-like in the imagery of Daniel 7. He is *human*. This Son of Man in Daniel 7 is the *ultimate* human who will rule as King of kings and Lord of lords *forever*.

This is how Jesus saw himself. And this is how Peter saw him too.

But do you see why Peter was so perplexed? How can the Son of Man suffer if he is sovereign? How can the Son of Man be rejected by rulers if he is *the* ruler? How can the Son of Man be killed if he is the King of kings? Peter could not see Jesus properly as the Son of Man who must suffer and die.

But perhaps we don't see Jesus properly as the Son of Man who sovereignly rules. When you hear of landslides, earthquakes, or tsunamis killing thousands of people, or suicide bombings, terrorist acts, and civil wars displacing millions, or abortions numbering as many as those who were murdered in the gas chambers of Adolf Hitler, it can be hard to believe that Jesus rules as the Son of Man. And when we live with the knowledge of sickness and death around us, it can lie like a shroud over life.

It can be hard to believe that Jesus rules as the Son of Man. And it can be hard to believe that he is doing anything about it. Have you ever felt this way?

But what we do know is that on one day in first-century Judea, the Romans crucified over one thousand people. But on another day, they crucified three. But it's not the one thousand who have the most significance, nor is it the three, but one of those three. And it's not that he died, because millions have died. It's not even that he died for a cause—because millions have died for a cause. World Wars I and II prove that. But it is that in this uniquely innocent human being who was fully God and fully man (the Son of Man), all the just anger of God the Father that should have been poured out on you and me, was poured out on him instead. He took upon himself the raging ocean of his Father's righteous wrath that *we* deserved!

But he didn't stay dead! He rose again on the third day as the Son of Man. Now he reigns supreme over every galaxy and every gene, every mountain and every molecule, every planet and every person, including you and me.

And every time we see Jesus heal someone, or raise the dead, or exorcise demons, or calm the storm, our eyes are opened to see what he foreshadows of the Kingdom he will finally usher in, when all things are made right. Each "miracle" in the Gospel accounts is when heaven and this fallen creation are transiently in sync to foreshadow Jesus' ultimate rule as the Son of Man. For he came to deal with sin and its effects once and for all through his life, death, resurrection, ascension, and return. This is the momentous news of the gospel!

And when we see Jesus properly it will compel us to obey him gladly. It will have radical implications for our lives. In Mark 8, Jesus goes on to say,

> "If anyone would come after me, let him *deny himself and take up his cross and follow me*. For whoever would save his life will lose it, but whoever loses his life for my sake and the gospel's will save it. For what does it profit a man to gain the whole world and forfeit his soul? For what can a man give in return for his soul? For whoever is ashamed of me and of my words in this adulterous and sinful generation, of him will the Son of Man also be ashamed when he comes in the glory of his Father with the holy angels." (Mark 8:34–38)

What does it mean to deny yourself? Does it mean denying anything pleasurable, like chocolate, or sleeping in, or an interesting movie? Does it mean not enjoying sex in a good marriage? Many monks in the monastic movement went this far. Some made vows to *never* enjoy the pleasures of this world. But it can't mean that because everything God created is good and is to be received with thanksgiving—food, marriage, and more (1 Tim. 4:4).

But to deny yourself is to deny everything that is *sinful* in yourself—to deny placing your own desires *above* God's desires. It is to shift your center of gravity from doing what is best for yourself to what is best for the glory of God. It is to deny your own selfish pleasures in favor of God's pleasures. Or to put it more positively, it is to make God's pleasures your own pleasures. And this is incredibly desirable if we see Jesus properly.

Furthermore, it means "taking up your cross." This image would have been shocking to first-century ears. There were three forms of execution in the first century—decapitation, burning, and crucifixion. Crucifixion was the most severe, and Roman citizens were exempt from undergoing such torture and shame.[24]

So to "take up your cross" evokes the picture of a condemned man who is forced to carry on his own back the cross-beam upon which he is to be nailed at his crucifixion. It is a shocking image of someone going out to die. It is the radical life of dying to your own *selfishness*.

As Don Carson often puts it, it is to live as if it is

- better to die than to lie
- better to die than to lack self-control
- better to die than to gossip
- better to die than to be unfaithful to your spouse
- better to die than to selfishly gain the whole world
- better to die than to be ashamed of Jesus

Jesus says, "What does it profit a man to gain the whole world and forfeit his life? For what can a man give in return for his life? But whoever loses his life for my sake and for the gospel will save it."

This is what it means to follow Jesus. It is to *gladly* lose your life for him.

To see Jesus properly as the Son of Man will compel us to gladly obey him forever.

If you claim to see Jesus properly, if you claim to be a Christian, then your life will look radical to this world, even though it is simply glad obedience to Jesus as the Son of Man.

He Saw Jesus

Howard Guinness saw Jesus properly. He was a medical student who accepted the invitation to go to Canada from the United Kingdom just after graduating. He bought a one-way ticket to proclaim the gospel on university campuses throughout Canada and then in Australia during the 1930s. He gave up his potential medical career and the prospect of gaining his fair share of "the whole world" for the sake of Jesus and his gospel.

In 1939, he wrote a little book called *Sacrifice*. In it he asks,

> Where are the young men and women of this generation who will hold their lives cheap and be faithful even unto death? Where are they who will lose their lives for Christ's, flinging them away for love of him? Where are those who will live dangerously, and be reckless in this service? Where are the men of prayer? Where are the men who count God's word of more importance to them than their daily food? Where are the men who, like Moses of old, commune with God face to face as a man speaks with his friend? Where are God's men in this day of power?[25]

Oh to see Jesus properly! It is a matter of life and death!

She Saw Jesus

My late wife Bronwyn also saw Jesus properly. She was diagnosed with end-stage pancreatic cancer in December 2009. But she never had any self-pity. She was only ever sad for me and our children because we would soon be without a wife and mother. Like you and me, she was a sinner. But she knew she had a great Lord and Savior in Jesus. And she cherished his gospel enough to continually pray for the nations. She never became a missionary. But as her body decayed over three painful years, she would almost always pray for unreached people groups in the Middle East as she lay in CT and PET scanners. She lived and died for the pleasure and glory of Jesus. And the day she died was March 31, 2013, Easter Sunday, the day we remember that Jesus rose from the dead to rule as the Son of Man!

Seeing Jesus properly will compel us to gladly obey him forever. Do you see Jesus properly? Let's close with these four questions.

1. Do you see Jesus properly as *your* Lord and Savior? Remember that even John Wesley didn't until he had already been on the mission field. It may be that you need to come before Jesus and ask him for forgiveness, and place your trust in him *alone* to save you from his just wrath to come. It will mean turning back to him as your Lord and Savior so that he becomes the pulsating center of your life.

2. Do you see Jesus properly so as to be done with sin? If we don't take sin seriously, we cannot be taking Jesus seriously. Remember to take up our cross is to live as if it is better to die than to sin. Do you delight in God's pleasures, or do you delight in your own sinful pleasures that you know displease him? We cannot be sinless this side of heaven. But do we take sin seriously enough to be killing it as God commands? (see Col. 3). If we live indifferently to sin in our lives, we cannot see Jesus properly. There is no point entertaining the thought of becoming a missionary overseas if you are not dealing with sin at home.

Do note that sin raises its ugly head in the most ordinary of circumstances. More missionaries return home because of quarrels with fellow missionaries rather than because of sickness or persecution. Killing your short temper with your family, or lack of self-control with your food, or impatience at the bus stop, or wrongful lust will only be desirable if we see Jesus properly.

3. Do you see Jesus properly so as to count yourself as nothing? When you sing, "Nothing in my hand I bring, simply to thy cross I cling," do you mean it? Do remember that the only thing we contribute to our salvation is our sin. So if we ever have the privilege of becoming a missionary, we must never think that God is lucky to have us on his team. In God's kindness, he may have gifted you with extraordinary gifts. But that is just what they are—*gifts*. And you were given them to use for *his* glory, not your own.

Like the centurion, we must recognize ourselves as *unworthy* before Jesus and gladly submit to his authority (Matt. 8:5–13). We can only bathe in his wonderful grace at the foot of the cross.

4. Do you see Jesus properly so as to share his joy in living and dying for the salvation of others? This is what compels us to be missionaries. It is to share his joy and pleasure in living and dying for the salvation of others. It is to care for all suffering but *especially* eternal suffering. It is to proclaim the glorious gospel of his Son and adorn this gospel through the fruit of good works.

Only in the gospel can we know that the glorious rule of Jesus means that nothing—not even cancer—happens at random. Only in the gospel can we bathe in God's love at the cross. Only in the gospel can we look forward to Jesus' return when his Kingdom intervenes to irreversibly destroy death. Only in the gospel can we see fellow sinners saved from hell.

Through gospel eyes, sin gets uglier, and grace gets bigger, Jesus gets greater, his death becomes more wonderful, and his resurrection gets more astounding. Although it does not remove our pain in this age, the gospel sustains us to seek and savor Jesus as the Christ in this age and the age to come.

What better news is there to proclaim? What better news is there to live and die for?

CHAPTER 6

The Call of God
Inspired, Informed, Confirmed

━━━━━ Mack Stiles ━━━━━

"God has called me to go with you to Guatemala!" So announced the voice on the other end of the phone.

I was happy to talk to this eager sophomore about the short-term program we directed in the highland of Guatemala. That same day I sent a packet of information to her about what we would be doing, where we would be going, and the requirements of any university student who applied.

Ours was no weeklong visit to the tourist city of Antigua, either. We hiked to villages recently burned in the Guatemalan civil war. We lived ruggedly, often spending our time days from the nearest city. There had been much death and murder in the Ixil area where we visited. It was a sobering place.

Not long after she received the packet of information that spelled out the nature of our trip, I got a second phone call.

"God has told me that I'm not to go to Guatemala."

Hmmm, I thought to myself, *her god's call to missions seems so capricious.*

What is the missionary call? A deep inner feeling? The parting of the sky? Something reserved for especially holy and spiritual people?

Too many would-be missionaries, and not a few missionaries themselves, spin out of the biblical orbit concerning missions because they have imbibed popular notions of missionaries and calling, rather than biblical ones. So we need to think through the missionary call by laying down some biblical principles.

It is helpful to get at the principles with four questions: 1) What is a missionary calling? 2) What inspires a missionary calling? 3) What most informs a missionary calling? and 4) Who confirms a missionary calling?

What's a Missionary Calling?

First, we need to define the word *missionary*. Admittedly, a definition of missionary is a bit arbitrary as the word *missionary* is not in the Bible. But I have a definition that comes from thinking about missionaries and watching actual missionaries close at hand for years: a missionary is someone who crosses a culture with the gospel to make disciples as their vocation.

Crossing cultures with the gospel to make disciples helps us sort out many who might call themselves missionaries but who are not, at least not in a biblical sense. For example, there are many Christians who happen to make a move cross-culturally for a job, or to follow family, but at the same time have no driving intent to make disciples. They are not missionaries. Put plainly, moving across a culture, or even living in another culture, does not make a Christian a missionary.

On the other hand, there are those who have jobs in a cross-cultural context looking nothing like the image of a traditional missionary, but who devote their lives to making disciples across cultures. They *are* missionaries. That's because their job serves a larger vocation, that they live to do, which is making disciples across cultures. We call them "tentmakers" after Paul's trade that he used to support himself as he ministered the gospel to unreached communities. I'm sure that Paul made very good tents, but his life calling, or vocation, was to preach to the nations.

Notice this definition guards us from two common errors we can make about missionaries. The first error is that all Christians are missionaries, something often touted from pulpits in the West, especially as we find ourselves in an increasingly post-Christian society. The second error is to see the missionary calling as such a holy calling it requires a special, specific, and personal direction from God for only very special people. Let's look at these two errors.

Not All Christians Are "Missionaries"

There's confusion about this because all Christians are called to live "on mission" where they are and to be involved in global "missions." After all, the final command of Jesus began with go into all the world (Matt. 28:18). This was not just for people who liked ethnic food. It was a command for all believers. Missions is simply another part of the Christian life, much like holiness. You don't say, "You know, I was working on holiness last week, but this week I'm going to work on something else."

Missions is the same way. We are *all* called to missions in some sense because missions is a part of being a Christian, but we're not all called to be "missionaries." To be called to missions is to be called to the global call of God. So in other words, all Christians have a calling to be active and intentional and willing to do missionary-like things in the Christian life, but not every Christian is a "missionary" in the strict sense, that is living cross-culturally to make disciples as a vocation.

So in Acts 13, for example, Paul and Barnabas were sent from the church of Antioch on a missionary journey. Everyone was unified in the mission, but not everyone from the church went with them, only Paul and Barnabas were "missionaries."

I like to think of it this way. If you have a friend with a headache, and you give them some Tylenol, it doesn't make you a doctor. You are simply doing something doctor-like.

So it is if you have a cross-cultural conversation, or a same-culture conversation, about the gospel; no one would call you a missionary in that case either. You are simply doing something missionary-like. So there is a distinction between missionaries and missions.

Missionaries Are Ordinary People

On the other hand, the second error is to think that missionaries have such a special calling that is so high and holy, that unless God splits the sky and speaks to us directly we *can't* be a missionary.

You don't need clouds to form your name in the sky; you don't need to hear a heavenly choir; you don't need to have a special identification with a region of the world; you don't need to be able to eat bugs; you don't need to tread the burning sands; you don't even need to feel goose bumps while reading this book (though that last one's pretty cool).

Being a missionary is a choice you can make about your life. You can prepare yourself for missionary service. You can grow and learn. In the freedom you have in Christ, you can aspire to be a missionary. But to do that you need to understand a *biblical* view of calling—what God means by "call."

Calling?

I believe we usually think the word *calling* a bit backward. Often, when we use the word *call*, we think of what we're going to do *for* God. But the Bible speaks more about our call as a calling *to* God. God is the one who calls us, or chooses us for himself, first for salvation.

So in Acts 2:21, Peter says, "Everyone who calls upon the name of the Lord shall be saved." There are thirty-nine uses of the word *calling* for salvation, in the New Testament like this. Not only that, but the ongoing sanctification in our lives is often described from God's viewpoint as a calling. There are twenty times in the New Testament where God calls us to live for him in a genuine way, with a changed heart. So, for example,

- Paul says, "God, who saved us and *called* us to a holy *calling* . . ." (2 Tim. 1:8–9).
- "God has not *called* us for impurity, but in holiness" (1 Thess. 4:7).
- "You were *called* to freedom, brothers. Only do not use your freedom as an opportunity for the flesh, but through love serve one another" (Gal. 5:13).
- "Walk in a manner worthy of the *calling* to which you have been *called*" (Eph. 4:1).

Michael Bennett, after his extensive survey of the word in the New Testament, says a "call" basically boils down to two things:

1. We are called to be Christians: God calls us to be genuine disciples of Christ as our Lord.
2. We are called to be holy and to grow in Christ-likeness: to be maturing disciples of Christ our Lord.[26]

That's our calling.

So, I can say with great confidence that I know the direction of God's call in your life. It's toward Jesus, always.

Now, you can do something really cool with this understanding. You can say things like, "I know God's calling in your life."

And they say, "Really?"

"Yeah," you say.

"Well, tell me!" they say.

"It's to be an ever-growing disciple of Jesus!"

Which might be a bit unsatisfying to your friend, but is actually the most important thing they could ever hear.

To see how backward our worldly understanding of the word *call* can be, look at this passage from 1 Corinthians 1:

> Consider your calling, brothers: not many of you were wise according to worldly standards, not many were powerful, not many were of noble birth. But God chose what is foolish in the world to shame the wise; God chose what is weak in the world to shame the strong; God chose what is low and despised in the world, even things that are not, to bring to nothing things that are, so that no human being might boast in the presence of God. (1 Cor. 1:26–29)

It's amazing to think that God's *calling* for us is to use us to demonstrate how great God is though our weakness and foolishness. We tend to think that we are attempting great things for God. But God understands that he is great, and we look pretty silly, and he uses that for his glory.

This is actually reassuring. You can look dumb, weak, and foolish as you faithfully follow Jesus, and you will be fulfilling your calling. Which sounds like the story of much of my life as I've bumbled along.

You might say to me, "I don't feel called to be an overseas missionary."

To which I can rightly say, "What's that got to do with it? Your feelings are not the sum total of your calling. There are other important things to consider." The fact is feelings are far too easy to confuse with our own sinful desires. This cuts both ways. Since this is a missions book, I suspect that many readers would say, "I *do* feel called to be a missionary."

Over the years, I've heard many people say they felt called to missions with nothing more than a feeling. So much so that nowadays a flag goes up in my mind when someone tells me they feel like God is calling them to be a missionary. That's because over the years I've discovered that people can go to the mission field for all kinds of bad reasons: escaping a bad relationship, a desire to see the world, they couldn't get a job when they graduated from seminary, and on and on. Their reasons can range from the trivial ("I just love Indian food!") to the very, very sad ("I'm going to do the hardest thing I can so that God will love me").

All had strong feeling they were supposed to be there. But a strong feeling does not make a call. Again, sinful desire is just too easily mistaken for a call.

The closest idea in the Bible that comes to dealing with a desire or feeling is when Paul affirms men who desire to be elders. In 1 Timothy 3:1, he says that to aspire to be an elder is to desire a noble thing. What Paul is clearly saying about people in leadership in the church is that their feelings are good when they desire to do a good thing. But Paul understood those aspirations to eldership to be conditional on a whole host of other things: how they treat their wives and children, how they handle the word, not to be a recent convert, and more. And notice that when he lists the requirements for elders (1 Tim. 3:2–7), having a deep inner feeling isn't in the list. So Paul is saying it's good for you to have a desire—wonderful. But your desire and your feelings are a starting point and not the entirety of your call.

This is a helpful pattern for would-be missionaries. To have a feeling of being a missionary to a certain place is a wonderful thing. Those of us on the founding and organizing team for the Cross conference have been praying for years that a conference like Cross, and a book like this, would stir your hearts to go to places where people have never heard the good news of Jesus. We want you to consider missions work as your life work—your vocation. And if that desire is raised in your heart, or freshly confirmed, as you read these pages, we are thrilled. But it's not enough, it's not sufficient, there is more that must be in place.

Inspired by God's Word

So, we've seen that a *missionary* is someone who crosses a culture with the gospel to make disciples as their vocation. We are *all* called to missions, because we are called to God and his heart is for all people, but not all people are to be "missionaries."

So if someone says, "I feel called to be a missionary," we say to them, "If you are a believer in Jesus, you are already called to missions, but your feelings are a starting point that must be confirmed by some other things to become a missionary."

So though our inspiration may start with our feelings, the far more important part of calling is that we would be inspired by the truth of what the Word of God says about missionary work.

It is very difficult to go any place in the Scriptures and not find a missions theme. From creation, to the fall, to redemption, to consummation—the arc of the story of the Bible points to the missionary heart of God. Ultimately what gives us inspiration is to see the heart of God in his Word, as his own Son "leaves home" in heaven and enters our world despite our broken sinfulness and the ultimate cost to him. From Genesis to Revelation, God shows us that he is on mission to rescue a people for himself and his glory. He is a missionary God. And he calls us to his mission.

As just one example, let's look at 2 Corinthians 5:10–19. I love this passage about ambassadorship. In it Paul is aiming to inspire believers with a vision for the world and our role in it; the very image of ambassadorship alone points to missions since ambassadors, by definition, don't live at home, but are "resident aliens."

Paul outlines in this passage four inspirations for missions. He starts by saying in verse 10 that judgment is coming for all people. So, a would-be missionary is inspired by what is at stake in people's lives. People are headed to hell; they are under judgment and will perish eternally if they do not hear the gospel and believe. And we have a prophetic role to persuade people that what God has ordained in judgment is true: judgment is coming; hell is real. So we move out in a hostile world to persuade people because we have compassion about their eternal destiny.

John Piper said at the 2010 Lausanne Congress on World Evangelization, "If you don't care for the poor, you have a defective heart, but if you don't care for the lost, you have a defective view of hell."

Notice, it's not only the coming judgment; it's the love of Jesus. Paul says, "Christ's love compels us" (v. 14 NIV 1984). What a beautiful thought. We are inspired by the love of Jesus. We want people to know of his fame, his glory, his awesomeness. Moreover, we see his love in our lives, and we long for others to know that he can do for them what he has done for us.

Of course, the world doesn't understand this. Paul understands that those who act in love look a little crazy. People thought that about Paul in verse 13, and they will think it about us too. We do look a bit crazy as we are controlled, or compelled, by the love of Christ. It's crazy love.

We're inspired by the coming judgment and Christ's love, but that's not all. Paul adds in verse 14 that we have concluded something: that Jesus died for all who would repent and come to him. We have concluded that sins can be forgiven, and reconciliation with God is possible though the death of Jesus. We've concluded that this man, Jesus, really rose from the dead. So we have in us the inspiration of the mind—the logical connection that this man Jesus who really rose from the dead has so proven the truth of the gospel that there is nothing he can ask of us that is too great a task.

And, furthermore, in verse 17, we understand the potential of what divinely created but fallen enemies of God can become: new creations in Christ, forgiven, restored, redeemed, re-creations from all around the world. Paul says this message has universal appeal, for all people at all times. Paul is not saying that all people will come to Jesus; he's not a universalist. He's saying that our message has universal appeal to all people. So the missionary call must be inspired with the idea that Christ's marvelous salvation is for the whole world.

These convictions lead us into a final inspiration, in verse 15: that Christ's death makes us alive to God; it *calls* us to live for others. So get your eyes off yourself, get your eyes off your circumstances, get your eyes off the things the world offers, and think about the call of God to God, and to his heart, and to his heart for the world.

So, in verses 10–19, we see how Paul lists these inspirations that serve as a guide for our call to missions: the fear of judgment, the love of Christ, our conviction of the universal truth of the message, our call to service. This potent combination propels us out in missionary ministry to serve others.

Here, in God's Word, we find our inspiration to step out of our safe worlds, to be committed and motivated, and driven to boldness, and even seeming craziness for those lost and without hope in the world. It's a call to throw away your life, as the world sees it.

So, to have a missionary call, we need to be inspired by God's Word. But we also need to have the missionary call informed.

Informed by the Gospel

A call to be a missionary must be informed by the gospel. That is, you understand that the work to be done in missionary service is the right proclamation of the gospel. And because the chief work of the missionary is the gospel, the way to evaluate all effort is a gospel ministry.

Yet an amazing number of people that call themselves missionaries, and desire to be missionaries, never share the gospel. There's much confusion about this in the Christian world, but I want to say it clearly: it is not the gospel to merely alleviate the needs of those in the world. As noble as it is to attend to the sick and hungry—they are worthy endeavors—without the message of the gospel, it is not missionary work. And it is a good indication that your "missionary" calling is not informed by the gospel.

But even those who desire to care for our neighbors as a right and good implication of the gospel (which I affirm) need to remember that the gospel, rightly proclaimed, does the best long-term good. Though modern academics use missionaries as punching bags, the mistakes of missions are largely anomalies, not the track record. Historically, wherever the gospel has gone, it has brought literacy and health, which secular historians rarely admit (and often owe their very jobs to).

I have seen this in my own experience. Missionary friends in Guatemala attempted to improve the living conditions of the Ixil people of the highlands. But it was not until the gospel changed hearts and brought revival that the Ixil people began to change the cultural difficulties that caused so many of the endemic problems of the communities: wife abuse, drunkenness, lack of education, even malnourishment.

One of the greater, more hidden, dangers in the missions world today is that much current missionary teaching and practice is informed by mere pragmatism, rather than the Christian gospel. For many, missions is seen as a pragmatic endeavor, a combination of the right strategy, language learning, cultural analysis, and cultural contextualization that will produce missionary success. But gospel advance is ultimately God's work, and we cannot put together a perfect strategy. His ways are bigger and better than ours.

I had a friend who recently attended a missionary gathering, and he said that there were many talks on mission trends, reports on missionary work, and one cultural analysis after another. But not one session or seminar about the gospel. Not one.

Let me quote him,

> There was no agreement about what the gospel is or isn't. The closest we came to talking about it was when we sang the few songs before each session. There was no room made to discuss it. I could only infer that because the gospel wasn't really discussed, it was absolutely assumed—and therefore not defined, celebrated, reveled in, and looked to for our motivation and goal in missions in the region. I was left wondering, where is the gospel? To work here, we need to agree on, be motivated by, and be guided by the gospel if we want to be faithful to God and his missionary purpose.

Do missionaries need to apply themselves to language learning and cultural sensitivity? Yes, of course. But we should never forget or underestimate the power of the gospel.

So, yes, we want to commend the gospel with works of service. But don't let the pressure of the world squeeze you into forgetting the gospel. Know it, live it, share it. Brothers and sisters, eat the gospel, breathe the gospel.

Paul says in Romans 1:16, "I am not ashamed of the gospel, for it is the power of God for salvation." The sad fact is many forget the power of the gospel when they go overseas.

Paul also says we must live in *line with the gospel* (Gal. 2:14). It's easy to think of the gospel as something that we move on from after we're saved. Don't untether the gospel from Christian living, your studies, marriage, or childrearing, Christian leadership, or missionary calling. Make sure the gospel is a part of all you do.

There have been times in my own life when I put my confidence in other things than the gospel: entertainment, social engagement, therapy. In my mind, somehow, I began to think that we could move on from the gospel. Somehow I had bought the lie that there was something bigger than the gospel, some higher ground. But we can't move on. There is no higher ground than the foot of the cross. All Christians, all pastors, all missionaries must stay firmly rooted in the gospel, for to step away from the gospel is a descent away from the cross.

Perhaps it dawns on you as you read this that you yourself are alienated from Christ. You should know that this gospel message is for you too. That you can be reconciled to a loving God, our Father, who sent his Son to pay the penalty for your sins on the cross so that you might be forgiven of sin and make peace with God. What's required of you is not to earn your way into his favor, but to repent of sin, especially the sin of unbelief, and turn to this resurrected Jesus in complete trust and faith.

So a missionary calling must be inspired by gospel principles that move us out in missionary service; a missionary calling must be informed by the gospel rather than those things the world tells us are essential, important as they may be.

Confirmed by the Church

It's helpful to understand church confirmation to missionary service by looking at three parts: love for the church, understanding of the church, sent by the church.

Love the Church

There are many who seem to hate Christ's bride. You can talk bad about me. But if you want me mad at you, start talking bad about my bride. In the same way, Christ's bride, the church, is very important to him.

Make it a habit to affirm both Christ's love for the church and your love for the church, since you want to love what Christ loves.

It's especially important to love the church since so many go to the nations with parachurch agencies.

The best way to demonstrate your love for the church is to join a church. Become a member. Take it seriously. You can't obey the New Testament commands to love other believers if you are not a member of the bride of Christ, the church. It's easy to love people theoretically. But it's when we're covenanted to real, live, flesh-and-blood sinners that we discover how real love is demonstrated. As Francis Schaeffer taught, our differences are not the end of love, but the occasion for love.[27]

Furthermore, you should never see the local church as something in competition with missionary work. I wish I had a dollar for every time I have heard an older missionary coach tell a younger missionary to avoid church involvement since it is a distraction to what they do. I was actually told not to become an elder as it would slow down student ministry. But my experience was very different; I found that as we plunged into church, God took care of the student ministry to which we were called.

Know the Church

So love the church, then know and understand the church as part of the confirmation for a missionary call.

Do you know what makes church *church*? Every aspiring missionary should have scriptural answers to that question. Just as few would deny the centrality of the gospel for missionaries, few would deny that church is central to God's missionary strategy. Yet when I talk with missionaries who are committed to church planting, they are often fuzzy about what a church is.

Can you define *church*? People who are attempting to establish churches as a part of the missionary mandate need to understand what a church is and isn't. Because it's so important to understand church, it's worth it to list them here.

What the Church Is: A local church is a gathering of baptized, born-again Christians who covenant together in love to meet regularly under the authority of the Scriptures, and the leadership of the elders, to worship God, be a visible image of the gospel, and ultimately, to give God glory (John 3:1–8; 13:34–35; Acts 2:41; 14:23; Eph. 3:10; Col. 3:16; 2 Tim. 3:16–17; Heb. 10:24–25).

What the Church Does: A church must do only a few things to be a church—the people regularly gather in gospel love to hear the word preached, sing, pray, give, and practice the sacraments of baptism and the Lord's Supper. Members, those who have covenanted together, lovingly care for one another (1 Cor. 12:12–26), including care through the practice of church discipline (Matt. 18:15–17).

The Mission of the Church: The church is God's strategic plan for evangelism with one overarching mission—to go to all peoples to make disciples, teaching them to obey everything Christ has commanded—including forming new churches (Matt. 28:18–20).

There it is: three key truths about the church in just four sentences, which takes less than a minute to say. This is the kind of thing every missionary should know well.

Sent by the Church

Finally, it's important to be sent by a church. Many self-confirmed missionaries show up on the mission field without any backing of a church; it's like baptizing yourself. The un-backed, lone-ranger missionary just isn't a biblical model.

The best test of a missionary call is that a healthy church agrees with your aspiration to be a missionary, affirms your skills and knowledge in ministry, gives you active positions in the church, and asks you to go with their blessing and support. Ultimately, the best way to understand calling is this: a church sends you out.

Unfortunately, too many seem to feel that simply moving overseas makes them a missionary, but there is nothing special about moving overseas. I wish it was that easy. I wish that getting on a plane would equip and confirm our call, but it can't and it won't.

Too many believe in what I call "the 747 principle": getting on a 747 changes you into a missionary. But understand this: if you aren't doing the work of ministry back home, you likely won't do it cross-culturally. Getting on a 747 isn't going to make you holy; getting on a 747 isn't going to make you a bold evangelist; getting on a 747 isn't going to make you a missionary. That needs to be something you practice no matter where you are, and that ministry is what is confirmed by a church, and frankly what is needed on the field.

So put an end to the practice of the self-assessed and self-confirmed missionary call, and make sure to go to your church for confirmation that springs from Word-based inspiration, gospel-centered information, and put into practice in a local congregation.

The fact is that ministry is actually harder to do cross-culturally. So, if you want to have a church affirm your call, you need to be a part of a church, and you need to take part in the leadership of the church. And if at all possible, it should be a church that's gospel-centered and healthy. The best way to reproduce a healthy church tomorrow is to be a part of one today. So be a part of a healthy church now. The mission field needs people who come from healthy churches and have seen them in operation.

So there it is: a missionary calling is inspired by God's Word, informed by the gospel of Christ, and confirmed by the church.

CHAPTER 7

The Life Worth Living for Christ Is a Life Worth Losing

━━━ Matt Chandler ━━━

Right now, all over the world, there are men and women who know nothing of Jesus Christ. They know nothing of the glory of the gospel, nothing of the good news. Yet God has providentially put a process in motion that will end in the proclamation of the gospel and, ultimately, their salvation. In places where we can't imagine, our God will reach out his hand and lay claim to his sons and daughters.

And in a crazy twist of "Take Your Kid to Work Day," God invites us into this plan. How crazy is that? Like the shepherds in the Nativity Story, we get to herald the good news. We get to lay down our lives, to suffer and to labor—it's a beautiful thing to give our lives to. As Paul writes in Philippians 1:21, "To me to live is Christ, and to die is gain." Or said another way, "A life worth living for Christ is a life worth losing."

The Arm of the Lord

The apostle Paul wrote these words. If you know much about Paul, you know that before he was an apostle, he was Saul of Tarsus and had a bit of a grimy reputation.

We see evidence of this in Acts 7 when Stephen gave a thunderous, non-seeker-friendly sermon out in Jerusalem—a sermon that enraged the crowd. *Enraged* is the correct word. They weren't just annoyed. They didn't just e-mail him the next day. There wasn't a heated debate on the Internet. Acts 7:58 says, "They cast him [Stephen] out of the city and stoned him. And the witnesses laid down their garments at the feet of a young man named Saul." Then just a few verses later, Acts 8:1 says, "Saul approved of his execution."

Notice Saul's reaction to the stoning of Stephen. He didn't see it as grotesque. It didn't shock or appall him. He wasn't wondering how he had gotten caught up in the mob. Acts tells us that he heartily agreed with the execution. He might have even enjoyed himself.

> Saul approved of his execution. And there arose on that day a great persecution against the church in Jerusalem, and they were all scattered throughout the regions of Judea and Samaria, except the apostles. Devout men buried Stephen and made great lamentation over him. But Saul was ravaging the church, and entering house after house, he dragged off men and women and committed them to prison. (Acts 8:1–3)

Saul of Tarsus gladly watched Stephen's execution. From there, he began to ravage the church, which means his approval of the stoning actually emboldened his rage against Christianity—so much so that he dragged people out of their houses and tossed them in prison.

In Acts 9, Saul's rage continued.

But Saul, still breathing threats and murder against the disciples of the Lord, went to the high priest and asked him for
letters to the synagogues at Damascus, so that if he found any
belonging to the Way, men or women, he might bring them
bound to Jerusalem. (Acts 9:1–2)

Saul's heart was dark. After his conversion, he described its darkness in stark terms, calling himself a blasphemer, a persecutor, and an
insolent opponent (1 Tim. 1:13).

We sometimes think of those who not only aren't interested in
the gospel, but are actually violent toward it, as unreachable. Instead,
we should think immediately of Paul. Is he not the objective evidence
that, no matter how dark the heart, God might reach, God might
save, God might deliver, God might transfer out of the domain of
darkness and into the kingdom of his beloved Son?

I've always marveled at that scene on the road to Damascus
because Paul certainly wasn't a seeker. On the road to Damascus,
he wasn't reading Tim Keller's *The Reason for God* or dialoguing
with someone who had just studied up on John Frame's *Apologetics
to the Glory of God*. He wasn't struggling with the truth of the gospel,
doubting his doubts. Paul was not the least bit worried about Jesus
as the Messiah.

And God was not the least bit worried about Paul. The Triune
God didn't lament, "What are we going to do? We had all these
plans for him, but he's not interested!" No. God knocked Saul off his
horse and blinded him.

Talk about electing love! Talk about a confidence that God can
save! This is the kind of love described by the prophet Isaiah when
he said the arm of the Lord is not too short to save (Isa. 59:1). God
doesn't have tiny T-rex arms. He can reach out and grab. He can
gather. He can hold to himself.

In his electing love, God reached out and grabbed the most violent, aggressive, rage-filled, anti-Christian man on record in the Scriptures during the first century. The long arm of God's saving love caused Saul to fall off his horse and fall hopelessly in love with Jesus Christ.

Those people are out there in the world—hearts still in darkness yet set apart before they were born—sons and daughters purchased by his blood. They will be found. They will be saved. They will be rescued. They will be ransomed. And he will use many of us—many Christians—to do that. We get to play a part. We get to go. We get to pray. We get to send. Every believer gets to be caught up in the mission.

What It Actually Means

It's easy for us to hear the words, "For me, to live is Christ," and miss their significance in light of Paul's story. We might even speak those words lightly ourselves. But Paul wrote those words out of the deep conviction that all other paths were bankrupt. At the church in Philippi, he became acquainted with Lydia, a woman of wealth and property. His team even stayed in her house. Yet he knew her wealth was bankrupt. He saw her wandering the outskirts of town searching for God.

Every day, the world attempts to disciple us into its view of what life is about. Commercials, movies, sitcoms, billboards, talk show hosts, and, yes, even some in Christian ministry tell us that the way to live is like Lydia did before Jesus: a life of toys and trinkets. The god of our generation is comfort. Suffering is seen as a problem to be solved, unless the solution itself is painful. Then we'd rather stay in our suffering. We don't want pain to free us from pain. We just want no pain.

From this perspective, suffering becomes problematic, not providential. God becomes this weak God in the heavens who's always huddling up the Trinity and saying, "Hey, who let that guy get cancer? Who let that woman get in an accident?" We have to be careful with this kind of thinking. It disciples us in the belief that comfort, wealth, trinkets, and toys are the sum of life.

Paul knew that everything was rubbish compared to the surpassing greatness of knowing Christ. *To live is Christ.* You might say it too, but you won't get it in your guts until, like Paul, you see the surpassing value of Jesus above and beyond everything else the unbelieving world exalts. Our culture exalts human relationships, achievement, skill. It says, "To live is my family, to live is my job, to live is my talent." It makes good things ultimate instead of letting good things point us to the ultimate good of Christ.

It's interesting that, for all the "to live is Christ" agreement among Christians, so little of our lives are actually about Christ. So little of our lives are actually shaped by him, informed by him, and driven by his Word.

We may say, "To live is Christ," but what we mean is, "To live is *my version of* Christ"—not the Jesus we find in the Bible but, instead, some god we create in our minds, some god that will make us "cool." But here's the thing: You're never going to be cool. It's junior high nonsense. May it die before you get in your late 20s or early 30s because it's incredibly sad to be 40 and still want to be cool. Jesus doesn't need a makeover. He's not meant to be hip. He's the Alpha and the Omega. He transcends that nonsense. To *live is Christ* means that we have seen the surpassing greatness of knowing Jesus above every other valuable thing known to man.

It's not that there aren't good things. It's not that there aren't blessings to be had or gifts given to us by God to be enjoyed. Of course, those things exist. But none are greater than Christ. Those gifts are given so that our worship and enjoyment of Christ might increase, and sometimes they are withheld so that our worship of Christ will stay where it should. In fact, Christ alone is worthy of an entire life's affection and devotion—and he's worthy of an eternity's more.

An Unordinary Idea

To die is gain. The idea is so out of the ordinary—nearly nonexistent in current streams of evangelical thought. I've never heard it addressed at any conference. Never heard it celebrated. Never heard it called precious in the eyes of the Lord. So few want to depart and be with him. But Paul said it because in his guts, he had seen the bankruptcy of everything else. He had seen the slavery in everything else—the total vanity.

And Paul wasn't being morbid or suicidal when he wrote those words. He wasn't disrespecting the life that God gave him. To understand that death is gain is to finally be free from fear in any capacity. The way to fullness of life is to understand that dying is gain.

In the second century, early Christian apologist Justin Martyr said, "You can kill us but cannot do us any real harm." What fearlessness we should walk in! What's the worst someone could do? Kill our bodies and torture us first? Yes. They could. That's true. But you have to believe that, in those moments, the Holy Spirit of God is present in profoundly powerful ways, as he has been throughout history.

In Hebrews 11, we see men conquering armies and shutting the mouths of lions. We see women receiving back their dead by resurrection. We see people who are tortured, cast out, and even sawn in half. We see Christians who are hard-pressed on every side, but the Holy Spirit is sufficient in the day of trouble. Throughout history, as men and women have been killed for loving Jesus, serving Jesus, and proclaiming the gospel, the Holy Spirit has sustained them in the day of trouble.

In her book *Shadow of the Almighty,* Elisabeth Elliot says, "Is the distinction between living for Christ and dying for him so great? Is not the second the logical conclusion of the first?" If Christ himself is our treasure, is it not the logical conclusion for us that our lives will be marked by him and our death viewed as a good thing on the day it occurs?

We don't die early. We don't die before our time. God knows all the days that he has for us. In 2 Corinthians 5:8, Paul says that we are of good courage because "we would rather be away from the body and at home with the Lord." Again, the Word of God thrusts this idea upon us: If Jesus is our ultimate treasure, then to depart from this body with all its limitations is a good thing.

A Better Day

For young and healthy people, the idea of death isn't even on the radar, except for those who struggle with misplaced fear and anxiety. Everyone agrees that *someone* will die this year, but no one thinks it's him or her. In reality, if Christ is our treasure, there should be no fear of death. And if to live is Christ and to die is gain, and to be absent from this body is to be present with Jesus, then we shouldn't be afraid to go. Ten thousand years from now, we won't be dreaming about the cool car we could have had if we'd lived just a little longer.

No. As Christians, we believe that a better day is coming. The better day isn't today. It isn't tomorrow. It might not even be a year from now or ten years from now. Eventually our weak and failing bodies will give way and go into the ground, and then at Christ's return, we will rise from the dead with new, imperishable bodies.

On the new earth, the wolf and the lamb will lie down together. The lion will chew hay like the oxen. The mountaintops will produce sweet wine. The deserts will bloom with roses. We'll have no need of the sun because the glory of the Lord and his presence will be our light. *To die is gain.* And we're getting closer to it every minute.

There's this profound passage in the Bible that's simultaneously beautiful and haunting—Revelation 6:8–11:

> And I looked, and behold, a pale horse! And its rider's name was Death, and Hades followed him. And they were given authority over a fourth of the earth, to kill with sword and with famine and with pestilence and by wild beasts of the earth. When he opened the fifth seal, I saw under the altar the souls of those who had been slain for the word of God and for the witness they had borne. They cried out with a loud voice, "O Sovereign Lord, holy and true, how long before you will judge and avenge our blood on those who dwell on the earth?" Then they were each given a white robe and told to rest a little longer, until the number of their fellow servants and their brothers should be complete, who were to be killed as they themselves had been.

The nations will be reached. They will be made glad in Jesus. The glory of God will cover the earth like the waters cover the seas. There are an appointed number of martyrs to achieve that, and not one martyr already under the altar has regrets. Not one is saying, "Lord, I didn't get to be married. I didn't get to walk my daughter down the aisle."

No, it's "How long until justice prevails? How long until your rule and reign is known by all? How long?" And the compassionate response from the King of glory is, *In a little while.* An appointed number of brothers and sisters will spill their blood to this end also.

Ravi Zacharias once talked about how ineffective it would be to threaten Lazarus after Jesus raised him from the dead. What would you say to intimidate him? "Hey, you're going to get yourself killed"?

He'd probably laugh. Similarly, the reason Paul was one of the most effective yet most frustrating missionaries the world has ever known is because his enemies couldn't do anything to him. *Put him in prison!* He's converting the imperial guards. *Beat him up!* He doesn't care. *Put him in the stocks!* He's singing songs. Imagine the frustration his torturers felt. If they let him live: "To live is Christ." If they killed him: "To die is gain."

Our Motivation and Treasure

But there's a flip side. Until Christ is our treasure, any other motivation for mission work becomes a fool's errand, built upon the motivations of man and not the call of God. That type of romanticism is doomed to fail.

Missions can become a kind of touchdown in the football game of faith, the end-all, be-all. "Where's the hardest place to go? The place no Christian survives? That's where I'm going—I win." Our motivation must be that Christ is the treasure, and that going there is out of glad obedience to Christ.

So ask yourself the hard questions. Is Christ truly your treasure? The heart is deceptive above all things. Is Jesus what you want, or are you trying to use Jesus to get what you want—to get to heaven, to get a spouse, to look respectable, or any number of other things?

Jesus urged his followers to have eyes to see that "the harvest is plentiful, but the laborers are few" (Matt. 9:37; Luke 10:2). In that verse, Jesus prays for more workers to be sent out. We too must ask him to do a work in our hearts so we might get to a place where we could gladly say, *To live is Christ, and to die is gain!*

We love our lives more than we should. We fear our death more than we should. We need the Father's help—to pray for a growing zeal for Jesus' name and renown. Where we have laid up other treasures, we must pray that Jesus crushes them. Where we have been seduced by lives of comfort and wealth, trinkets and toys, we must pray that God would free us from seduction. Where we have bought into the idea of "cool," we must repent. May we treasure him above all things.

Workers *are* needed in the harvest, and some of them will receive the title not just of *worker*, but of *martyr*. I pray that we would not love our lives more than we love God. Imagine five hundred years from now, five thousand years from now, ten thousand years from now, how trite and silly the luxuries of today will seem! Let us be motivated by his love, for his glory, through his transformative grace.

Right now, in the hardest places in the world, among the most unreached of peoples, the Father has sons and daughters. They will be saved. He will gather them. And we should be humbled and overwhelmed to be invited in, to participate in the greatest mission the universe will ever know.

Victory is sure because it has already been secured by the shed blood of Christ. May men and women from every tribe, tongue, and nation on earth pour out their time, energies, talents, giftings, passions—their very lives—for this mission. To live is Christ, and in him, to die is truly gain.

CHAPTER 8

Give a Dam for Jesus

━━━━━ Michael Oh ━━━━━

I don't use this title lightly, and I don't want to be provocative simply for the sake of being provocative. But I think this title expresses a very important message, and alternative ways to say it, like "Give a hoot for Jesus," just didn't seem to get it across.

And let me further explain the background of this phrase, which may not have anything to do with profanity at all. Some understand the phrase to have originated about 150–200 years ago.

The rupee is the base currency in India today, worth about 1.5 cents. But originally the rupee was a silver coin. It was worth less than the gold mohur coin, but more than the old copper coin, which was called a dam.

I have a dam coin from the year 1517 and another from 1497, which dates them back five hundred years. The copper dam coin was in use during the British occupation of India, and to the British soldiers of that day, was virtually valueless.

So apparently when British soldiers were in the marketplace, people tried to sell them shoddy goods, and they would sometimes respond, "I wouldn't give a dam for that!"—meaning they wouldn't pay even a single dam for goods like that. Eventually the phrase took on the nuance, "I don't care about that."

So in this chapter, I want to talk about some important things that we should care about, namely, the gospel, suffering, and missions. And I want to look at suffering around the world and help us think together about how we should view that suffering and how we should respond to it.

What if God's people gave a dam about suffering? What if God's people gave a dam about the gospel? And stopped giving such a dam about money, reputation, success, what you drive, where you live, what you look like, who likes you, or anything else that isn't worth giving a dam for.

The average age of children exploited and enslaved into prostitution globally is said to be twelve to fourteen years of age. Some six hundred thousand to eight hundred thousand women, children, and men are bought and sold across international borders every year and exploited for forced labor or commercial sex. When internally trafficked victims are added to the estimates, the number of victims annually is in the range of two to four million. Fifty percent of the victims are estimated to be children.

Do we give a dam?

The Call to Be Prophetic

A Chinese leader recently said, "The church needs to be a prophet and a servant." Very simply put, a prophet could be described as one called to see circumstances as God sees them and to speak into those circumstances God's message and truth to his people and to the world. And today the church, the people of God, has opportunity to be prophetic in a few different ways.

We can be prophetic when we look at the world and see suffering and injustice and say, "That is wrong! That is so wrong!" And say it not just amongst ourselves, but to the world.

We can be prophetic when we explain from God's Word why it's so wrong. Why such wrong is offensive to the God who created people in his image. Why such wrong is offensive to the God who is holy and merciful and compassionate. And when we explain the good, true, honorable, right, just ways and standards of God.

Because we have the Bible, every Christian has the opportunity to speak God's word and ways forth prophetically into the church and into society and our world. And to be prophetic not just about things that society would agree with, but to speak truth and God's honor about all that he calls us to speak.

And when you're faithful in that prophetic speaking of God's word, I think that's when you have those moments of realizing, "Oh! That's why so many prophets of old were killed!" In Micah 2:6, we see the people's opposition to prophetic word: "'Do not preach'— thus they preach—'one should not preach of such things.'"

But Christians are to speak out about and care about all forms of suffering and injustice—poverty, racism, sex trafficking, homelessness, exploitation, or like Micah 2, preaching against materialism and oppression of the poor by the rich.

And when we do this, it is a wonderful witness of the compassion of the church. Society will even applaud this championing of these very right causes. But they won't necessarily applaud our giving a dam about other kinds of injustices and heartaches and sins.

What are some of the sufferings and injustices that God would have us preach and prophesy about that the world around us doesn't care to hear about and would respond with, "Do not preach such things!" Or simply, "Do not preach!"

In America, each year, 1.2 million unborn children are lost through abortion—their lives snuffed out, strangled, stolen. Globally

40 million lives were lost this year alone. More than 1 billion unborn children have been murdered in the last 30 years.

Christians are to speak prophetically against injustices and sins like abortion, homosexual practice, and materialism with teaching from the Word of God, from the perspective of God, speaking into society, resisting opposition, enduring ridicule for the alleviation of all kinds of suffering and injustice on earth. We need to do it with love, with humility, with integrity, and we need to do it with boldness and urgency.

The Call to Be Servants

Along with being prophetic, we as the church of Jesus Christ have the opportunity, the calling, to be servants. In other words, to give a dam about such suffering by doing something about it.

Servants meet the practical needs of others. So as the church, we should be involved in the freeing of slaves, in the protecting of the weak, in the clothing of the naked, in the housing of the homeless, in the adopting of orphans, in the righting of wrongs.

We are to speak prophetically and serve as servants those who are suffering and are in need: "He defends the cause of the fatherless and the widow, and loves the alien, giving him food and clothing. And you are to love those who are aliens, for you yourselves were aliens in Egypt" (Deut. 10:18–19 NIV 1984). We are to serve the needs, alleviate the suffering of the fatherless, the widow, and aliens, sojourners, foreigners, strangers.

There are almost one million international students and scholars around the world who have left their homeland to study and teach in North America. There are many of them on your campus, if you will just look for them. Many of them are the top scholars and future leaders of their nations. Globally 86 percent of Buddhists, Hindus, and Muslims don't personally know a Christian. But so many international students are from Buddhist, Muslim, and Hindu nations—the very core of the unreached peoples of the world.

Did you know that most of the international students on your campuses will never enter a home while in America? What if you and your family gave a dam? To be a friend to an international student. To invite them into your home over break. To invite them to your church. To invite them into your life. You are to love those who are aliens, for yourselves were aliens.

God cares about all kinds of suffering and so should we.

It's estimated that because of gender-based infanticide, abortion, malnutrition, and neglect, there are 160 million females "missing" from the world's population. According to a ministry called She Is Safe, in the Nuwakot district of Nepal, there are whole villages with no girls over the age of twelve. All have been sold by fathers, brothers, and uncles.

Sushmita was sold for less than $100 to a trafficker when she was nine, presumably for a "good job" in India. Upon arrival she was drugged and raped to prepare her for a life of prostitution. Her forced labor included flights to the Middle East, as a high-priced girl. She was also used by her captors to go back to Nepal to tell girls what a fine life she had in India and to recruit them as sex slaves.

In one year alone, an estimated twelve thousand girls were trafficked from Nepal to the brothels of India. It is estimated that one hundred thousand Nepali women and girls work in brothels in Mumbai alone. Fifty percent of these have the HIV virus. There are three million prostitutes in India. Forty percent are young girls. Globally there are between twenty and thirty million people living as slaves.

And personally my heart breaks for North Korea. A United Nations panel heard testimony of a North Korean woman forced to drown her baby in a bucket. Children are born into prison camps and never know of the world outside. Prisoners are surviving on rodents, grasshoppers, lizards, and grass. They scavenge through excrement for morsels of food. Eight out of every ten women who escape North Korea reportedly end up being exploited in prostitution.

We need to give a dam for these people.

The Call to Suffer

Let me shift gears a bit and make another point about suffering.

Not everyone wants to be rescued from every type of suffering. This particularly applies to Christians. And it's not always God's purpose to rescue everyone from every kind of suffering. And part of the Kingdom ethic may rightly and gloriously cause some Christians to increase their exposure to suffering for the sake of the alleviation of the suffering of others.

What do I mean? There is intense, deadly, pervasive, diabolical persecution of Christians going on around the world. I have dear friends in Africa, Asia, and the Middle East who have experienced imprisonment, attack, burning of houses and churches, and have witnessed the death of friends. There is a political advocacy that we should work toward. A way to show that we give a dam. There are important legal and political processes and advocacy that are right and God-honoring.

We need to find ways to release pastors from prison. We need to find ways to help get Saeed Abedini released from prison in Iran. We need to advocate on behalf of Beijing Shouwang Church pastor Tianming who has been under house arrest for more than three years. We need to advocate for religious freedoms in China and North Africa.

But I can also say that not a single one of my friends sees political rescue as the end goal or even as the necessary purpose of God for their nation or people. Some Chinese friends of mine said to me, "Don't pray for China to open. Pray for us to be faithful. And for

God to be glorified through our suffering." God sometimes chooses to use persecution and suffering for his glory.

I have a dear friend Alemu who is a key leader in Ethiopia. He has faced execution-style death and survived by nothing short of angelic intervention. That suffering has shaped his life and leadership, impacting mine as well.

There can be redemptive purposes in suffering. This is true for non-Christians as well. How many glorious testimonies have been told by those who have suffered, have cried out to God for mercy, and received the forgiveness of their sins and the rescue of their souls? Of course, suffering is not a blessing in and of itself, but suffering can be a blessing if it can somehow heighten the understanding of the reality of our need for God.

Blessed are those who know their emptiness, their need, their pain. But toward their rescue—earthly and heavenly—Christians need to be with, stand with, and serve those who are suffering. Christians must be there to compassionately point out the lessons of pain and point to the ultimate solution to pain in Christ.

Suffering for Christians can also be redemptive for others. The biblical Kingdom ethic and eternal perspective on life may rightly and gloriously cause some Christians to increase their exposure to suffering for the sake of alleviating the suffering of others.

Why is this not *insane*? Or why is such *insanity* rational? Why would a Christian choose to be less comfortable, less wealthy, less safe for the sake of others whom they don't even know? Because Jesus Christ has already rescued us perfectly and eternally from the greatest possible suffering. Jesus has rescued us from our sin, rescued us from eternal separation from God; therefore we can choose to suffer lesser suffering—poverty, persecution, loss of family, friends, culture, comfort, finances—that others might have their rescue.

This is not a reckless exposure to suffering but intentional, missional, and glorious. Jesus' rescue of your life eternally is what makes moving into a bad neighborhood sane. It's what makes the insanity of generous, sacrificial giving to actually be sane. It's what makes adopting a special needs child sane. It's what makes the insanity of "throwing away your life" for missions sane.

Fellow Christians, you can choose to suffer earthly suffering because Christ has already rescued you from the greatest possible suffering. And you can choose to suffer earthly suffering and to sacrifice earthly sacrifices because through your life, through the gospel, through your presence, through your comfort of others, others who are suffering can come to know an eternal comfort and blessing.

Jesus took up his cross to show mercy and give salvation for sinners. He calls us in turn to take up our crosses, that others might receive mercy and salvation.

Change the World

One thing I love about this new generation of young adults is that there is such a desire to impact our world. And that's true not just of Christians but the whole generation. But what I want to challenge us to think about is, what does world impact or changing the world look like for a Christian and from an eternal perspective?

A lot of young people might say, "Yeah, I give a dam about suffering. See these shoes? They're Toms." "Yeah I care—and somebody is wearing a free pair of shoes somewhere in the world because of me." "Changing the world one pair of shoes at a time, baby!"

But as you look at your peers and look into your own heart, I just want you to know that changing the world is not as easy as some would have you think. It takes more than clicking "Like" for a good cause to change the world. Of course, it may look different from generation to generation, but what will stay the same is that making a difference costs, and costs dearly.

I was in Johannesburg, South Africa, in December 2013 to participate in Nelson Mandela's memorial service as one of twenty religious leaders who had been invited to join the family on the platform. And as I sat there praying in the rain with tens of thousands of South Africans dancing and mourning and laughing and singing around the stadium, there were so many things going through my mind. We may not all agree about Nelson Mandela, about his methods or his morality. And I didn't know the man personally, but I think we can pretty much all agree that he gave a dam. He gave a dam about freedom. And he gave a dam to fight against racism, poverty, and oppression. And he didn't just say that he gave a dam, but spent twenty-seven years of his life in prison because of what he believed.

Mandela's words before the court at the infamous Rivonia Trial in 1964, which he thought were very likely his last words before being condemned to death, stirred my heart as I read them on the plane to Africa.

> During my lifetime I have dedicated my life to this struggle of the African people. I have fought against white domination, and I have fought against black domination. I have cherished the ideal of a democratic and free society in which all persons will live together in harmony and with equal opportunities. It is an ideal for which I hope to live for and to see realized. But, my Lord, if it needs be, it is an ideal for which I am prepared to die.

Is there anything in your life that you are willing to die for? Is there anything in life that is worth dying for? That's what we need to figure out and do something about. It might look different for different people. The world needs Christians who will live out the gospel in every sphere of society—in politics, business, law, sports, medicine, arts, engineering, education, and more. The world needs Christians who live boldly on behalf of every sphere of society—for the poor, for the oppressed, for the uneducated, the fatherless, even defending the proper rights of the unworthy.

What if Mandela had been an evangelical Christian and open about his faith and the impact of the gospel in his life? What if he had fought for the rights of the oppressed on gospel conviction and both lived the gospel and shared the gospel? His life impact could have been eternal and heavenly rather than "just" an incredible impact here on earth for a long, long time.

This world needs Christians who will stand for Jesus and stand for people—Christians who will represent Christ to the world for both earthly and heavenly good, for both temporary and eternal good. If—when—we give a dam about all kinds of horrible, horrible suffering in this world, when the world sees and knows that Christians give a dam, our witness is strengthened and we have greater opportunity and greater integrity and greater credibility to share the gospel.

But mute witnesses (even those who do good) fail in their witness if they do not share and speak of and explain and advocate and appeal for the gospel, those who give cool water but who mute the name of Jesus. Dietrich Bonhoeffer taught, *Silence in the face of evil is itself evil. Not to speak is to speak. Not to act is to act.* Advocates for various causes rightly challenge people on the injustice of doing nothing. That is true and right for many causes. But how great an injustice it is to know about eternal suffering and do nothing. How great an injustice it is to know about hell and not help a single soul go to heaven.

Why do we need to give utmost attention to sharing the gospel? Because we want those who are suffering, and all people, to have Jesus. Anything less than knowing Jesus is not enough! It's not enough to just know satisfaction from hunger, not enough for people to know their ABCs, not enough to drink clean water, not enough to have a home, not enough to be freed from slavery, not enough to be trained in a skill. We want them to know and worship and love and adore Jesus!

Some people talk about holistic ministry, but what they seem to mean is physical care without the gospel. We need to have holistic ministries of justice and rescue and advocacy. But to be truly integral and integrated, they must deal with the spirit, the soul, and give people a chance to hear the gospel and respond to the gospel. If we don't share with them what can save them for eternity and what will allow them to know Jesus, we don't really give a dam. Or we don't give a dam if they are damned.

Another wrong is when we speak the gospel but live lives that belie our beliefs. This too is a failure in our witness for the gospel. There are those who speak in Jesus' name, but curse it through their actions and character and lives. Those who call themselves champions for justice, but live unrighteous lives. A champion for ending the sex trade, but a slave to pornography. A champion for viral movements for Jesus, but not even praying. A champion for saving the world, but not sharing the gospel with your classmates or friends. A champion for Jesus on Twitter, but not in your neighborhood. A champion for ending poverty, but a chump to materialism. And you don't give a dam, a penny, for God's greatest cause. Those who speak the gospel but neglect to live out transformational lives, being both transformed by the gospel and acting as gospel agents, fail in their witness for the gospel.

Another failure in our witness for the gospel is when we live half-hearted Christian lives. Anyone who wants to find flaws in Mandela's life and put them on display will find them. But one lesson that rang deeply in my heart when I was in South Africa was that we all have something to learn from him. I only wish for myself and other Christians to live as courageous and conviction-filled a life as his, especially for eternal causes.

To live sparingly for the right cause with the right theology is nothing to be proud of. We are to love and cherish and enjoy all that we have in the grace of God. But we are not to abuse it nor use it as an excuse to live half-heartedly for Jesus. Jesus deserves and demands all of who we are and the whole of your life, and honestly I don't think there's a better way to live that life than as a missionary. It is one of the greatest privileges of my life to be a missionary.

My Own Story

My own calling to missions starts with the story of suffering—the suffering of my family. My father was born in 1936 into a Korea that was not free. No, not North Korea, but the whole nation that was under the control of Japanese imperialism. My father, Sung Kyu Oh, was born with the name Hideo Matsuyama, a Japanese name, as a subject of the Japanese Emperor.

My great-aunt was married off as a young teenager to avoid becoming one of two hundred thousand so-called "comfort women"—sex slaves of the Japanese Imperial Army—women and girls as young as twelve years old who endured rape dozens of times per day. In the thirty-plus years of Japanese Imperialism in Asia, an estimated thirty million lives were lost. So my calling to Japanese missions began not with compassion for their poor or to help provide clean water, but a difficult call to obey Christ's command to *love my enemies* with great hope to see my former enemies become my brothers and sisters through the gospel.

And I want you to know that God is at work in Japan, one of the largest unreached people groups in the world! The ministry continues to be difficult in what many consider to be the most difficult mission field on the planet. But we are seeing a wonderful season of fruit-bearing in Japan. Our seminary, Christ Bible Seminary, has almost tripled in size over the past few years. Future leaders are being trained for the Japanese church.

I had the privilege of baptizing seven people in April 2013 for our church plant. We're ready for our next round of baptisms. We've had college students pray to receive Christ right on the first floor of the seminary in our Heart & Soul Café. And yes, I'm still in Japan serving as a missionary. After I accepted the invitation to serve as director of the Lausanne Movement, I was asked, "When are you moving to America?" I replied, "I'm not. Lausanne is moving to Japan!"

The missionary life is not glamorous. It's pretty mundane at times, except when it's painful. But it's an incredible blessing to be a part of something that really does change the world and really does make an impact that lasts forever.

So why don't we have more missionaries? I think one big reason is that we believe we'll be happier doing other things and that being a missionary is kind of miserable. You have to raise financial support. Miserable. You have to leave your family. Miserable. You have to learn a new language and culture. Miserable. And you have to learn to get along with complete strangers on your team whom you don't even get to choose. Potentially quite miserable.

But James 1:17 says, "Every good and perfect gift is from above, coming down from the Father of the heavenly lights" (NIV 1984). J. C. Ryle talks about how if this is true, then there is no blessing found in sin. If there was a good gift in sin, it would have to come from God, and no sin comes from God. So stop thinking that somehow those in sin are to be envied or anyone apart from Christ is to be envied or that anything anyone has apart from Christ is to be the right object of your longing or affection.

Missions also is very much about obedience. And that's a pretty unpopular message today. Ryle says, "We think that we would be absolutely miserable obeying God. That was the devil's argument in his temptation of Eve, but it is as diabolical now as it was then." And

I think there are a lot of people who think the same way about missions. Will there be suffering? Yes, absolutely! Will you be miserable in obeying God? Absolutely not!

If we turn away from such good, the goodness of such obedience in missions, we're not turning toward happiness but away from it. Do not say, as Ryle warns, "If I live for God, I'll lose out." You may lose out on the things that don't last, that do not satisfy, that do not feed your soul; but you will gain things eternal, things that satisfy, things that feed your soul. You will gain more and more of Christ.

If you give a dam, would you consider giving your life as a missionary?

Not Everyone Is a Missionary

You may have a few days, from time to time, of human regret as a missionary. But you'll celebrate the fruit for ten thousand times ten thousand years! But whether missionary or not, all Christians are to be a part of God's mission in this world and the mission of the church. That doesn't mean that everyone is a missionary. As has been written very clearly in this book, *not* everyone is a missionary. But all Christians are to be a part of God's mission in this world.

We obey locally (as evangelists and those who live as salt and light in our societies), and we send globally, sending missionaries to those who have not heard. All of us are to play the role of senders. There is no Christian who should not be a sender. Romans 10:14–15 gives some insight about the role of missionaries and senders:

How then will they call on him in whom they have not believed? And how are they to believe in him of whom they have never heard? And how are they to hear without someone preaching? And how are they to preach unless they are sent?

As it is written, "How beautiful are the feet of those who preach the good news!'"

So, first of all, we have those who have never heard the good news. They are to be a priority. There is to be urgency about reaching such people.

One of the key concepts and strategies for global missions today is unreached people groups (UPGs). This was introduced at the first Lausanne Congress in 1974. An unreached people group is a distinct ethno-linguistic people that has less than a two percent evangelical Christian population and less than five percent Christian adherents. According to the Joshua Project, today there are more than seven thousand unreached people groups in the world, which amount to almost three billion people.[28] More than six thousand of the UPGs are in the "10/40 Window"—a rectangular region of North Africa, the Middle East, and Asia from about the 10 degree north latitude to 40 degrees north. This mission strategy was introduced by Luis Bush at the second Lausanne Congress in 1989.

Nearly three thousand of these unreached people groups are *completely* unengaged. That means that there is not a single church, not a single mission *agency*, that has taken responsibility for that unreached people group. There is no gospel witness at all. Within these three thousand unengaged, unreached people groups, there are 533 of them with populations more than twenty-five thousand. Might there be 533 people reading this chapter that God would raise up to engage those 533 unengaged, unreached people groups?

Romans 10:14 says that people cannot believe in him of whom they have never heard. And also that they cannot hear without someone speaking the gospel. So there is a personal communication that is essential to belief in the gospel. This is where the missionary comes in. Missionaries have this distinct privilege and responsibility to bring good news to those who have never heard. And for those who hear and believe, we have the glorious promise of Romans 10:13 that "everyone who calls on the name of the Lord will be saved."

Sent

Then we have Romans 10:15, "And how are they to preach unless they are sent?" So we learn here that missionaries are those who go somewhere, especially to those who have never heard. And also that they are sent, and this is clearly the role of the church, of all of us. How do we send? Biblically speaking, I think we can point to at least two concrete ways.

First, in this passage we see that missionaries are sent as those who are cherished: "How beautiful are the feet of those who bring good news!" We should see missionaries—plain, awkward, weak, sinful, insecure, poorly dressed missionaries—and think, *Beautiful!* How beautiful are the feet of those who bring good news. Rather than be annoyed or disturbed when a missionary comes to you or your church asking for help or financial support or to be housed or prayed for, we should welcome them, love them, and cherish them.

And a second biblical way to send is through giving a dam. A vitally important way to love and cherish missionaries is through financial giving. And I'll tell you, I really think that talking about money and giving is one of the least popular topics for Christians today. Want to know the quickest way to lose followers on Twitter? I've figured it out. Ask people to give money. If you ask for money to fight trafficking, it's actually okay. You'll gain some followers. But if you ask for missions giving, I guarantee you will lose followers.

Jesus lost followers talking about money too. But that didn't stop him from preaching about money. Jesus' ministry was financially supported by believers. Paul requested financial support for gospel ministries. Paul also received support for his mission journeys.

The apostle John tells us how to treat missionaries in 3 John 6–7 (NIV 2011): "Please send them on their way in a manner that honors God. It was for the sake of the Name that they went out, receiving no help from the pagans." Mark 12:41–44 (NIV 2011) says,

> Jesus sat down opposite the place where the offerings were put and watched the crowd putting their money into the temple treasury. Many rich people threw in large amounts. But a poor widow came and put in two very small copper coins, worth only a few cents.
>
> Calling his disciples to him, Jesus said, "Truly I tell you, this poor widow has put more into the treasury than all the others. They all gave out of their wealth; but she, out of her poverty, put in everything—all she had to live on."

The widow of Mark 12 gave a dam—she gave two dams—putting in her two copper coins for God. Hers is the example of the extravagant giving of little, the little that was her all. It was a costly, worship-filled giving. Not long ago, I received an e-mail about a donation for the Lausanne Movement from a pastor in Dar es Salaam. He wrote,

> FROM TANZANIA ALL TANZANIANS LIVE ON UNDER $2 PER DAY ON AVERAGE. WE NEED PRAYER AND GOOD LEADERS TO MOVE FORWARD.
> THE RICH BECOME RICHER AND THE POOR ARE TOO POOR. I AM LEADING A CHURCH WITH JUST 120 BELIEVERS.
> I AM SENDING FOR LAUSANNE $300.

That's like an American church of 120 people sending a $30,000 offering. We all need to be challenged by the extravagant giving of little by the poor. And others, many of us, are called to the extravagant giving of much. Like the pouring of perfume upon Jesus' head in Mark 14—which was 300 denarii worth, and would be more than $30,000 today.

Give

Let me encourage you now, whether you're a college student or done with school, to commit to giving at least ten percent for the church and at least ten percent for reaching the unreached. Ultimately, giving is a heart issue. If you give a dam, you'll give a dam. If you don't give a dam, you won't give dam.

There is also a lifestyle issue because generosity is enabled and empowered by financial stewardship and lifestyle simplicity. The less you spend on other things temporal, the more you have to spend on things eternal. But that too is a heart issue, isn't it?

Too many of us, it seems, have lost the understanding and theology of giving as worship. Giving to the church and giving for missions is worship to God! But instead we've learned from this world that we are sovereign individuals (accountable to no one) who act as sovereign consumers. We assume that we are sovereign individuals who exercise sovereign decision-making as sovereign investors, whether stocks, cars, fashion, electronics, houses, or retirement. Instead, giving should be an act of worship by submitted stewards to a worthy Lord. Every dollar spent is a vote on value. It's an act of worship; what's important to me, what I love.

If you give a dam about people created in the image of God; if you give a dam about eternal salvation or eternal damnation; if you give a dam about the adoration and worship of God; if you give a dam about the gospel; if you give a dam about God, then give. Give a dam. Give two dams—even up to your last two coins' worth.

What's at stake here? What's the ultimate opportunity and what's the cost? Because there is a cost. It's costly to give a dam. It's costly to try to make a difference. It's costly to preach. It's costly to live prophetically. It's costly to care about hell and talk about it openly and do something about it. But it's even more unbelievably costly for those who go to hell.

Hell and damnation are not apart from God. The purpose and existence of hell is not evil. And damnation is not evil. God has absolute, holy authority over hell and damnation. As Virginia Stem Owens wrote in the *Reformed Journal* years ago,

> Let us get this one thing straight. God can do anything he damn well pleases, including damn well. And if it pleases him to damn, then it is done, *ipso facto,* well. God's activity is what it is. There isn't anything else. Without it there would be no being, including human beings presuming to judge the Creator of everything that is.[29]

The reality of God's absolute authority and also the reality of eternal damnation are absolutely stunning and humbling and convicting. It leaves us with nothing but the plea of mercy.

Jesus says in Luke 12:5, "I will warn you whom to fear: fear him who, after he has killed, has authority to cast into hell." God has authority to send to hell, and he does so justly and mysteriously as well to his glory. We should not speak casually about hell. And we must not be silent about hell either. That would be unjust. It is unjust to not give a dam about damnation.

So let's give a dam. And let's be faithful in the whole of our gospel witness. Biblical witness bearing is:

Holistic, all-encompassing, sufferers embracing,
life transforming, and persecution facing;

Person activating, orally explaining,
detail expressing, intellectually engaging;

Salvation-in-Jesus adoring,
cross-of-Christ bearing, repentance imploring;

Response demanding, sanctification inciting,
never-the-same rejoicing, hands-feet-mind-mouth inviting;

"Jesus is the *only* way to heaven" declaring,
"God have mercy on me" shouting, and testimony sharing;

Grace and mercy extending, suffering alleviating,
"I'll suffer with you, I'll suffer for you" sacrifice instigating;

"I'll go to the ends of the earth for you, Lord" insanity
    producing,
"Be reconciled to God" proclaiming, Christ exalting and me
    reducing;

"I'll lay down my life for you" demonstrating,
"Here are my last two coins" giving motivating;

Reality of hell recognizing, eternal suffering warning,
new home in heaven with no more death, pain, or mourning;

In light of eternity, urgency inspiring,
proclamation and demonstration of the God who's worth
    desiring.

Christ's invitation to us to take up our crosses is the call to suffer
and sacrifice. Would you increase your suffering and sacrifice for the

alleviation of others' suffering? Would you do it as a love offering to the Lord?

Suffering Earthly and Eternally

What can we understand about earthly suffering? It's unavoidable. It can be alleviated either in degree or duration. It's temporary. It's sometimes unjust and sometimes undeserved. It always has the potential to be instructive. And it can be redeemable, if those who suffer can learn the lessons of pain and the solution to pain in Christ. Redeemable if those who suffer can find the greatest blessing of knowing Jesus. And if we give a dam, we'll do something about earthly suffering, as the church, for the Lord's glory and for the good of the world.

How about eternal suffering? Unlike earthly suffering, eternal suffering is avoidable. It cannot be alleviated either in degree or duration. It's eternal. Irreversible. It's always just and deserved. And those who enter into eternal suffering are beyond redemption.

So if we give a dam, we'll do something about it, as the church, for the Lord's glory and for the good of the world. While we still can.

CHAPTER 9

The Church as the Means and Goal of Missions

══ D. A. Carson ══

Dear friends, let us love one another, for love comes from God. Everyone who loves has been born of God and knows God. Whoever does not love does not know God, because God is love. This is how God showed his love among us: He sent his one and only Son into the world that we might live through him. This is love: not that we loved God, but that he loved us and sent his Son as an atoning sacrifice for our sins. Dear friends, since God so loved us, we also ought to love one another. No one has ever seen God; but if we love one another, God lives in us and his love is made complete in us. This is how we know that we live in him and he in us: He has given us of his Spirit. And we have seen and testify that the Father has sent his Son to be the Savior of the world. If anyone acknowledges that Jesus is the Son of God, God lives in them and they in God. And so we know and rely on the love God has for us.

(1 John 4:7–16)

It is common to begin a sermon, or a chapter of a book, with a relatively brief introduction and then devote most of the time, or space, to unpacking and applying the assigned biblical text. Certainly, that is what I usually do. In this case, however, I am going to begin with a fairly lengthy introduction, followed by a fairly brief treatment of the passage I have just read. The reasons will become clear below.

In this introduction, I ask two questions: *(1) What does sin do?* (Not, *What is sin?* But, *What does sin do?*); and *(2) What does the gospel do?*

What Does Sin Do?

Sin Defies God

That is the way it was in the account of the Fall in Genesis 3. The serpent asks, "Did God really say, 'You must not eat from any tree in the garden'?" (Gen. 3:1). Or again: "God knows that when you eat from it your eyes will be opened, and you will be like God, knowing good and evil" (Gen. 3:5). So instead of taking God at his word, our first parents are enticed into thinking that they can stand over against him and adopt an alternative perspective. Sin begins with defying God.

Those who sin greatly often learn that the person they have most greatly offended is the living God. Recall how David seduced his neighbor Bathsheba. She became pregnant. Her husband was at the battlefront, fighting one of David's skirmishes. She let David know that she had become pregnant by him. David thought this mess might yet be covered up. He sent word to the front through his military channels and had Uriah the Hittite, Bathsheba's husband, returned to Jerusalem, ostensibly to carry a military message back to the commander-in-chief. David thought to himself: *You know, he'll go home and sleep with his wife, and if the baby comes a little early, well, things like that happen—a preemie who's a little big for being a preemie, but it will do.* But as it turned out, Uriah was so concerned to be identified with his mates at the front that he didn't return home to all of home's comforts. He slept in the palace courtyard, expecting to return to the front the next day. David knew he was snookered. So he sent another message to his military commanders, this time carried by the hand of Uriah himself—this honorable man who was carrying his own death sentence. The commanders arranged a little skirmish and gave everyone else in the platoon except Uriah a code word that signaled retreat. The inevitable happened. At the decisive moment, his mates fell back, and he was left at the sharp end and was killed.

David thinks he has got away with it. In due course, however, he is confronted by Nathan the prophet. As shame and guilt begin to wash over him, in deep contrition David writes Psalm 51. Addressing God, one of the things he writes in that psalm is this (v. 4): "Against you, you only, have I sinned and done what is evil in your sight." Of course, on one level that is not true. David certainly sinned against Bathsheba—he seduced her. He sinned against Uriah—he had him killed. He sinned against the military high command—he corrupted them. He sinned against his own family—he betrayed them. He sinned against the nation, for as chief magistrate he was pledged to uphold justice. In fact, it is hard to think of anybody that he did *not* sin against. Yet he dares say to God, "Against you, you only, have I sinned and done what is evil in your sight."

Here David displays massive insight, for in the ultimate sense what makes sin so awful, what makes sin so terrible, what makes sin so fundamentally wretched, so heinous, is that it is an offense against God. Sin defies God.

Earlier in 1 John 3:4, John writes, "Sin is lawlessness." Some commentators insist that this is a pathetically shallow definition. But it all depends on who gives the law. If John is claiming that sin is merely a matter of breaking arbitrary rules, then his definition is indeed pretty shallow. But if sin is not doing what God commands and doing what God forbids, then the definition "sin is lawlessness" is invested with spectacular weight. Sin takes on an element of heinousness, of opprobrium, of malevolence that is measured by defying God Almighty, by wretchedly abandoning the glory and the grace of God.

Elsewhere, there are other definitions of sin, but they are all tied to God. "Everything that does not come from faith is sin" (Rom. 14:23). But this is faith in God. "If anyone, then, knows the good they ought to do and doesn't do it, it is sin for them" (James 4:17), we are told elsewhere. But what is good? Good is what is aligned with the mind and the purposes and the will of God. What is the first commandment? To love God with heart and soul and mind and strength. So the fundamental sin is not to love God with heart and soul and mind and strength. Sin defies God.

Sin Utterly Corrupts Each Individual

This does not mean that each of us is as bad as he or she could be. Believe it or not, each of us could be a little worse. But the point, made again and again in Scripture, is that every dimension of our existence has become twisted—our thought, our emotion, our wills, our memory, our imagination, our fantasy life, our priorities, our goals. This is why Paul can write, in Romans 3, in words largely drawn from the Old Testament,

> As it is written: "There is no one righteous, not even one; there is no one who understands; there is no one who seeks God. All have turned away, they have together become worthless; there is no one who does good, not even one." "Their throats are open graves; their tongues practice deceit." "The poison of vipers is on their lips." "Their mouths are full of cursing and bitterness."

"Their feet are swift to shed blood; ruin and misery mark their ways, and the way of peace they do not know." "There is no fear of God before their eyes." (Rom. 3:10–18)

In other words, sin utterly corrupts each individual, so much so that even when we do "good" things, the "good" deeds are enmeshed in self-focus. We listen to a little voice that says to us, "See, you're doing something good. That proves that preachers who focus on sin the way they do are simply nasty and narrow. You're good!" Pretty soon our good deeds are awash in specious self-congratulation. By contrast, the Bible says that even our righteous acts are like filthy rags (Isa. 64:6). Sin utterly corrupts us.

Sin Corrodes All Social Relationships

That too starts in Genesis 3 when God confronts Adam. Adam immediately replies, in effect: "Well, it's not my fault. I mean, you're the one who gave me Eve. You might have given me a better woman." This is not the last man to blame his wife. Of course, she is no better: "You know it wasn't my fault. The devil made me do it." Thus they display their shame. And because they are ashamed, they have so much to hide—that's why they want to cover up. When you are perfectly open and clean, when there is nothing to hide because there is no two-facedness or deceit, when every thought, imagined image, and word are kind and true, reflecting who you are at the deepest level of your being, then there is nothing to hide. But already Adam and Eve are hiding; they have to cover up. Would you like your dearest friend or family member to know absolutely everything you think and imagine? God help us. All of us have so much to hide *from one another*. This is the measure of the corruption of our social relationships.

The social relationships that break down are in our families, on our streets, everywhere. Marriage so often becomes a one-upmanship—you always have to put the other person down. It's a competition, a striving for power, unkind words.

And then, there are the private sins that corrode social relationships. Jealousy—which, nevertheless, affects how you view other people. Porn—you think that's private, but as a result, you view the opposite sex in horrible ways, and it begins to affect your relationships, ultimately in marriage itself, how you rear your children, where your sense of humor is, and what you value. The lust for power, for respect, for control, for wealth, for advantage, even when we're lusting after things that can be good, are so often bound up with wanting to be on top. The test is when we pursue these things, do we pursue them with equal passion for others or primarily for ourselves. The second commandment in importance, after all, is love your neighbor as yourself.

Sin corrodes all social relationships.

Sin Issues in Death

First of all, we experience death toward God. We are dead to him; we do not know him. We run from him, as did our first parents in Genesis 3. And of course we are destined to experience physical death. We tend to become more alert to this reality when we travel through war and plague. After all, we have just come through the bloodiest century in human history. One reads with glassy eyes the poem by Carl Sandburg, written after the slaughter of World War I: "Bury the dead at Ypres and Verdun. I am the grass. Let me work." But that was followed by World War II and Auchswitz, by millions more killed in China and the Ukraine and in tribal savageries in Africa, by mass slaughter in Cambodia of between a quarter and a third of the population. Yet all those shocking deaths miss the point, for, in any case, we all die. The death rate has not gone up. It has been one hundred percent for quite a long time.

But that's not the final death. The Bible speaks of the second death (Rev. 20:11–15).

Sin issues in death.

Now that's my answer to the first question, "What does sin do?" Sin defies God, it utterly corrupts each individual, it corrodes all social relationships, and it issues in death.

What Does the Gospel Do?

We want to remember, of course, what the gospel *is*. The gospel is, first of all, news. That's why what you do with it is proclaim it. That's what you do with news: you proclaim it. The gospel is specific news: it is news about what God has done in Christ Jesus—supremely in his cross and resurrection—to address all the wretchedness of sin. That's why we read, for example, Paul's concise definition in 1 Corinthians 15:1–4:

> Now, brothers and sisters, I want to remind you of the gospel I preached to you, which you have taken your stand. By this gospel you are saved *[that is, saved from sin and all of its dimensions effects],* if you hold firmly to the word I preached to you. Otherwise, you have believed in vain. For what I received I passed on to you as of first importance: that Christ died for our sins according to the Scriptures, that he was buried, that he was raised on the third day according to the Scriptures.

When you work your way through the rest of 1 Corinthians 15, you discover that the gospel is biblical; it is God-centered; it is Christ-centered; it is cross-centered; it is resurrection-centered. It is news to be announced and expounded to men and women everywhere. That is what the gospel *is*.

But what does the gospel *do?* The gospel abundantly answers and overturns everything that sin does. This is what the gospel *does*. In particular:

The Gospel Reconciles Men and Women to God

That is why Christians focus so much on justification. God who is alienated from us by his own standards of holiness, who because of our sin stands against us in judgment and wrath, nevertheless pursues us in love so as to reconcile us to himself. He actually dares to call us "just," not because we are, but because he sent his Son to bear the penalty of our sin—the curse of our sin. In the gospel, the good news of what God has done in Christ Jesus, supremely in his cross and resurrection, Christ's righteousness is counted to us and our sin is counted to him. He cancels the sin—he expiates it. He propitiates his own Father—he makes him favorable toward us so that there is no residue of judgment left hanging over our heads. Because of what Christ has done by the Father's wise and gracious plan, God declares us to be just; he justifies us. Thus the gospel reconciles men and women to God. If God is thus restored to the center of our lives, then he is glorified. The gospel reconciles men and women to God.

The Gospel Utterly Transforms Believers

That is why the new birth is so important. Salvation is more than justification. Justification settles our status before God, but in itself it does not change us. But the gospel changes us; it transforms us in this life, and transforms us perfectly in the new heaven and the new earth.

We would not believe apart from God's work in our lives by his Spirit. This is not to be confused with simply turning over a new leaf, by resolving to try harder. That is why Christian conversion is always different from Muslim conversion or Buddhist conversion. In the Muslim understanding of conversion, conversion finally turns on an act of will. You decide to follow Allah and his prophet. You commit yourself to the five pillars of Islam. This is your choice. Once you have made that choice, you have converted to Islam. But although Christian conversion certainly involves the will, it involves more than that. It involves regeneration. God so works in us by his Spirit that we gain a new origin, a new beginning, a new starting place. This new birth, as Jesus calls it, can be thought of as being born of water and Spirit (John 3:1–5). The language is drawn from Ezekiel 36 where God promises a new covenant characterized by water and Spirit—water that symbolizes the cleansing of human beings and Spirit to reflect the power of transformation. This new birth, this conversion, is a cleaning up, a miraculous transformation. Everyone genuinely "converted" has been the subject of a miracle that has been brought about by God himself. The gospel utterly transforms believers. In consequence, we act differently. That brings us to a third thing the gospel does.

The Gospel Renews Social Relationships

The gospel establishes a new humanity. It establishes a new covenantal community, a new family. In other words, it does more than transform individuals into some sort of loose aggregate; it unites them together into a new organism, a new family, a new covenant community, a new humanity, a new body. So much is this the case that this new family transcends in importance our natural families; the Lord Jesus goes so far as to say, "Everyone who has left houses or brothers or sisters or father or mother or wife or children or fields for my sake will receive a hundred times as much and will inherit eternal life" (Matt. 19:29).

When I was an undergraduate at McGill University, there was an orthodox Jewish young man who became a Christian. His parents held a funeral for him and forbade him to have anything to do with the rest of his natural family. But God raised up a family for this young man—a new family, a new body.

Biblical passages that make the same point are rich and diverse. For example, in Matthew 16, Jesus does not say, "I will bring many individuals to me," although he will, but "I will build my church" (Matt. 16:18). Paul tells us, "Christ loved the church and gave himself up for her" (Eph. 5:25). Or consider that the apostle draws a contrast in Galatians 5 between the acts of the flesh and the fruit of the Spirit. Observe how many of the acts of the flesh are corrosive of social relationships: "The acts of the flesh are obvious: sexual immorality, impurity and debauchery *[the first three focus on the sexual arena, which, whether in act or imagination, focuses on other people];* idolatry and witchcraft *[these two overflow with anti-God paganism—and both are normally practiced with others];* hatred, discord, jealousy, fits of rage, selfish ambition, dissensions, factions and envy *[the biggest sector of the list—and all have to do with social relationships];* drunkenness, orgies, and the like *[absolute dissipation, rarely practiced in isolation].* I warn you, as I did before, that those who live like this will not inherit the kingdom of God" (Gal. 5:19–21).

But if the acts of the flesh are social, so also is the fruit of the Spirit: "The fruit of the Spirit is love, joy, peace, forbearance, kindness, goodness, faithfulness, gentleness and self-control" (Gal. 5:22–23). The gospel renews social relationships. Begin with the first entry in this list of the fruit of the Spirit: "The fruit of the spirit is love"; you can't love on your own, in splendid isolation. To love, there has to be "other." This is one of the reasons why the doctrine of the Trinity is so important in biblically-faithful Christianity. In

Islam, Allah is often referred to as the All-Compassionate and the Merciful; his sovereignty is often magnified. But almost never is he declared to be loving. In what sense could the solitary Allah, in eternity past, love? But the Bible insists that in eternity past, God loved the Son, and the Son loved the Father. In the complex oneness of our Triune God, there is always "other." And now, shall we be converted as individuals and have no "other" to love? The fruit of the Spirit is love. In this we are to reflect the very nature of God.

The other elements of the fruit of the Spirit likewise testify to the reality that the gospel renews social relationships. Joy is rarely an isolated emotion. Because we are social beings, joy erupts in a network of fulfilling relationships, both with God and with his image bearers. Peace transcends mere personal tranquility. It includes peace with God, and peace with others. Forbearance gladly puts up with things, and puts up with people, in a spirit of gentleness. Similarly, neither kindness nor goodness can be displayed when there is no "other." Kindness leavens every relationship. Even in marriage, it is perhaps the greatest aphrodisiac. Faithfulness, gentleness, and self-control, the last three entries in this list of the fruit of the Spirit, can, I suppose, be expressed in private tasks when you are entirely isolated from other people, but their greatest exemplification occurs in your relationships with other people.

Consider another passage penned by Paul. In the body imagery found in 1 Corinthians 12, he reminds us that the body is made up of different parts working together. The body of Christ is not one big eyeball or one big toenail. It is a body with different parts, all working together. The gospel that constitutes this body renews social relationships.

One more passage: in Ephesians 4:17 and following, Paul briefly tells us what it means to be transformed. Those who are unconverted are "darkened in their understanding and separated from the life of God because of the ignorance that is in them due to the hardening of their hearts" (Eph. 4:18). Verses 20–21: "That, however, is not the way of life you learned when you heard about Christ and were taught in him in accordance with the truth that is in Jesus." And then a little further on, the social dimensions are worked out:

> Each of you must put off falsehood and speak truthfully to your neighbor, for we are all members of one body. "In your anger do not sin": Do not let the sun go down while you are still angry, and do not give the devil a foothold. Anyone who has been stealing must steal no longer, but must work, doing something useful with their own hands, that they may have something to share with those in need. (Eph. 4:25–28)

Do you hear all these social dimensions?

> Do not let any unwholesome talk come out of your mouths, but only what is helpful for building others up according to their needs, that it may benefit those who listen. And do not grieve the Holy Spirit of God, with whom you were sealed for the day of redemption. Get rid of all bitterness, rage and anger, brawling and slander, along with every form of malice. Be kind and compassionate to one another, forgiving each other, just as in Christ God forgave you. Follow God's example, therefore, as dearly loved children and walk in the way of love, just as Christ loved us and gave himself up for us as a fragrant offering and sacrifice to God. But among you there must not be even a hint of sexual immorality, or of any kind of impurity, or of greed, because these are improper for God's holy people. Nor should there be obscenity, foolish talk or coarse joking, which are out of place, but rather thanksgiving. (Eph. 4:29–5:4)

Do you get the picture? There is a social dimension to what this gospel does. It does more than save you from hell, as important as that is. That is why the Bible dares to affirm that "the church of the living God" is "the pillar and foundation of the truth" (1 Tim. 3:15). In other words, we stand firm, a pillar and a foundation in a world that is restless, unstable, sliding around in disarray. The church herself is designed by God to be stable, like a steadfast pillar, a foundation when shifting sands give way. That is more than organizational stability. It is stability that is built up because the gospel itself renews social relationships, enabling us to mirror the gospel. Thus we become the foundation of the truth.

Roman Catholics have often loved the little Latin formula *extra ecclesiam nulla salus:* "Outside the Church, there is no salvation." As they use it, of course, the phrase suggests that outside the Roman Catholic Church there is no salvation. But there is a sense in which Reformed Christians will gladly repeat the saying, even though they mean something different. "Outside the church, there is no salvation"—for the church is the community of the blood-bought. It is inconceivable in the first century that someone would say: "Yes, I've become a Christian, but I don't want to join a church. You know, I'm not for institutionalized religion." It is simply inconceivable.

The Gospel Kills Death

The gospel kills death in all of its dimensions. We are brought back into a living community with a living God: we are no longer dead to him. We anticipate resurrection existence in the new heaven and the new earth. Already eternal life is pulsing within us. It is not just that individuals gain eternal life, but an entire transformed community radiates the life of eternity, the life of God. Ultimately we look forward to a new heaven and a new earth, the home of righteousness, where there will be no more death or sorrow or pain or tears or deceit or sin of any kind. And that's just the negative side of holiness. There, we will love God with heart and soul and mind and strength, and our neighbors as ourselves. Our lives will redound with praise to the glory of God. God will be all in all, and we'll love it. All of this comes to us because the gospel kills death.

Now let me draw some strands together before we come to our passage. We have seen what sin does. It defies God. It utterly corrupts each individual. It corrodes all social relationships. And it issues in death. We have seen what the gospel does. It reconciles men and women to God. It utterly transforms believers. It renews social relationships. And it kills death. Obviously, the second list matches the first list. Now, the topic assigned to me is "The Church as the Means and the Goal of Mission." Transparently, this focuses on the third element of each of my two lists: sin corrodes all social relationships, and the gospel renews social relationships.

But we must now perceive two unavoidable lessons that fall out of what we have learned from this survey.

(1) In order to foster clarity, we talk about one element in each list at a time, but it is important to see that they all hang together. Yes, sin defies God, but it simultaneously corrupts individuals, destroys social relationships, and issues in death. Similarly with respect to the gospel: the gospel simultaneously reconciles us sinners to God, transforms, renews social relationships, and destroys death. Because of debates that dominate this or that particular period in history, there may be a need to stress one element more than another—for example, we might lay special emphasis on justification, our status before God. So it was at the Reformation. In another period of history, the Great Awakening at the time of Whitefield and Wesley, there was a substantial emphasis on new birth. Strictly speaking, however, mature Christian thinking demands that we grasp that, even though justification and the new birth are distinguishable, they must never

be radically divided, and neither may legitimately be ignored or underplayed.

Similarly, we dare not think of salvation in purely individualistic categories that ignore the social dimensions of the gospel—any more than we may think of salvation as only for this life and forget that ultimately our hope is in a new heaven and a new earth, the kingdom still to be consummated. Seeking reconciliation with God and the glory of God must not be set over against the centrality of the church. Or conversely, the importance of the church and of planting churches must not be set over against the transformation of individuals. So although I am about to focus now on the church as the means and goal of mission, we must not overlook all the dimensions of the gospel.

(2) But I do want to focus on the church as the means and goal of mission. The second lesson, then, is that salvation must be thought of in more than individualistic categories. Paul, for example, not only evangelizes—that is, he preaches the gospel in new places to see people converted—but he seeks to establish churches. So important is this to him that when he goes out on his first missionary expedition, authorized and sanctioned by the church at Antioch, after preaching the gospel in place after place, he returns home by working backward on the same route. Instead of going to new towns and working his way back again by another route, as he certainly well could have done, he reverses course and stops in all the places where he had been in order to assure himself that these communities, these fledgling churches, were well governed, that they had elders, that they were being disciplined, that the doctrine was sound. He is interested not only in the salvation of individuals, but in the establishment of the church.

So now, at last, I finish my introduction, and we come to 1 John 4:7–16. What does this passage add to our topic? Our passage displays two great themes. The first is the completion or the perfection of the love of God in the church—that is, the church as the goal of mission. And the second is the revelation of God in the church—that is, the church as the means of mission.

First Theme: The Completion of the Love of God in the Church—the Goal of Mission (vv. 7–12)

I will go through the logical flow of John's argument in seven steps.

Step 1. He begins with an exhortation to Christians to love one another (v. 7a). "Dear friends, let us love one another."

Step 2. Such love, he asserts, flows from regeneration. "Dear friends, let us love one another, for love comes from God. Everyone who loves has been born of God and knows God. Whoever does not love does not know God, because God is love" (4:7–8).

Step 3. John discloses that the ultimate paradigm of love, the ultimate display of love, is God himself (vv. 7–8). "Whoever does not love does not know God, because God is love" (4:8).

Step 4. This love from God is shown specifically in the sending of his Son Jesus. "This is how God showed his love among us: He sent his one and only Son into the world that we might live through him" (4:9).

Step 5. John establishes that this love of God is most powerfully displayed not merely in the Son's coming, that is, in his incarnation, but in Christ's cross-work on our behalf. God "loved us and sent his Son as an atoning sacrifice for our sins" (4:10). Christmas is never enough; it is followed by Good Friday and Easter. This expression "atoning sacrifice for our sins" has been variously translated, but as far as I can see, it means something like this: In the cross, Christ voluntarily took my place, bearing the guilt and punishment that my sins deserved, dying my death, so that the sin is canceled, and the offense of our sin has so been removed that God no longer stands over against me in wrath but in favor. Christ's death cancels the sin of his blood-bought people (that's what Christians have called *expiation*) and thus turns aside God's righteous wrath (that's what Christians have called *propitiation*).

The fact is that God stands over against us in wrath because of his justice and holiness in the light of our sin. And he stands over us in love because he is that kind of God. And God thus demonstrates his love by sending his Son to be the sacrifice that cancels sin and propitiates the Father. He is the perfect sacrifice of atonement. He is the expiation and the propitiation for our sins. This is the unimaginably great demonstration of God's love, a love superbly summarized in a verse all Christians learn by heart: "God so loved the world that he gave his one and only Son" (John 3:16).

Step 6. John now tightens his argument by verbalizing the "ought": "Dear friends, since God so loved us, we also *ought* to love one another" (4:11). To fully grasp John's point, it is worth pausing for a moment to remind ourselves of what John's first letter is about. First John was written to a church or to churches that were being barraged by certain kinds of errors. In the course of his response, the apostle keeps reiterating that real Christians display three virtues: a passionate commitment to the truth, especially the truth as to who Jesus is and what he has done; a determined resolution to obey God's imperatives; and a self-sacrificing resolve to love one another.

So there's a truth test, a moral test, and a love test—and it's not "best two out of three." All three are important; all three are essential. And then in chapters four and five, as the letter draws to a close, John wraps these three tests together in one. Instead of presenting three individual tests, John shows that they all hang or fall together.

So in our passage, watch how John brings these tests together. We are to love one another. That's the love test. But the highest demonstration of love is found in God sending his Son—and this, of course, demands that we confess who Jesus is. That's the truth test. But note the *ought* in the argument: "Dear friends, since God so loved us, we also *ought* to love one another (4:11). We *ought* to do this. That's the obedience test. And as you read from here all the way down to 5:12, you discover that these three things are tied together again and again.

Step 7. John asserts that all of this works toward the completion of God's love in us. Initially, the language is astounding: "No one has ever seen God; but if we love one another, God lives in us and his love is made *complete* in us" (4:12). What? Was God's love incomplete before? Or some versions have "and his love is perfected in us." What? Does that mean his love was imperfect before? No, not quite. God cannot do something extra or additional to enlarge or complete or perfect his love. The supreme demonstration of his love is precisely in the gift of his Son which takes him from Christmas to Good Friday to Easter, from the incarnation to substitutionary atonement to triumphant resurrection. God so loved us that he gave his Son. Yet the very purpose of that love is that it should reach out and so transform the redeemed that the very love of God is fleshed out in the church. It is fleshed out in people. And in that sense, it comes to its fullness, its goal, its purpose. It is not that God himself was lacking in love, and now we have added something to it so that God's love is a little richer now. Rather, its very purpose is the transformation of his redeemed people, so that they, too, love. In that sense, as we reflect the love of God himself, God's love is completed in us.

To think in purely individualistic terms is too small a vision. The completion of the love of God in the church is the very goal of mission.

Second Theme: The Revelation of God in the Church—the Means of Mission (vv. 12–16)

We now focus on verses 12–16. Notice how verse 12 is transitional: "No one has ever seen God; but if we love one another, God lives in us and his love is made complete in us." What does the first clause contribute to the argument? "No one has ever seen God." Suppose we were to remove those words: what would be lost? Why don't we read, more simply: "Dear friends, since God so loved us, we also ought to love one another " (v. 11). And "if we love one another, God lives in us" (v. 12). What is verse 12 adding?

John reminds his readers that we human beings—broken, fallen, sinful, sin-cursed human beings—cannot gaze on God and live. The angels that surround the throne cover their faces with their wings. How much more must we be protected from the sheer glory of perfect holiness in the face of God. When Moses says to God, "Show me your glory" (Exod. 33:18), God says no one can see his face and live (33:20). He eventually allows Moses to see something of the trailing edge of the afterglow of his glory, and to hear God intoning truly wonderful words (34:6–7). But no more than that. No one can see his face and live.

And then, in the fullness of time, God sends his Son. The evening before he is crucified, one of his disciples says to him: "Show us the Father and that will be enough for us" (John 14:8). Jesus replies, "Don't you know me, Philip, even after I have been among you such a long time? Anyone who has seen me has seen the Father. How can you say, 'Show us the Father'?" (14:9).

That is why Christians sing at Christmas:

Veiled in flesh the Godhead see;
Hail the incarnate Deity.
Pleased as man with men to dwell—
Jesus our Emmanuel.

That's as close as human beings are going to come to seeing God until the end of the age when Christ himself is revealed in the matchless glory of the noonday sun, the time when his blood-bought people have so been transformed that they will be able to gaze on him who sits on the throne, and the Lamb, and be intoxicated by the unshielded glory.

How, then, shall people see God today? Verse 12 insists, "No one has ever seen God." No one. But then John adds, "but if we love one another, God lives in us and his love is made complete in us" (1 John 4:12). In other words, in some measure we Christians are displaying him. After all, did not Jesus himself say: "By this everyone will know that you are my disciples, if you love one another" (John 13:35)? Do you see? The revelation of God in the church, not least in our love, is the way God discloses himself to a watching world. The church is God's means of mission.

All the remainder of these verses down to verse 16 keep reiterating and establishing that point. It is enough here to point out a couple of details. In verse 14, John tells his readers, "We have seen and testify that the Father has sent his Son to be the Savior of the world." So we—here an inclusive "we," we Christians—are bearing witness to the truth. We are telling the truth; we are gospelling; we are evangelizing. Out of love, we bear witness to the reality that the Father out of love has sent his Son to be the Savior of the world. And the result? "If anyone acknowledges that Jesus is the Son of God, God lives in them and they in God" (4:15). In other words, the love that is displayed among us is not of the sentimental, squishy type that has no substance or defined action. Rather, it displays in such concern for the world that we testify to the grace of God, to the glory of God, to the incarnation and to the cross-work, in the hope that others will acknowledge that Jesus is the Son of God, and in turn share in this Spirit-imparted eternal life. So we are impelled, as a community of believers who love one another, to proclaim the gospel because of love—in the first instance, because of his love for us. This is how "we know and rely on the love God has for us" (4:16). Here is the church as the means of mission.

In the sweeping redemptive purposes of God, God has ordained to bring glory to himself by reconciling this condemned universe back to himself. He is undertaking this work by the means of the cross. That cross-work has as its aim the establishment of the blood-bought church of the living God. The completion of the love of God in the church is the very goal of mission. But as God's love is displayed in the church, the church is God's own witness now—God's own means now of proclaiming the gospel by word and by transformed life.

The church that Jesus is building is both the goal and the means of mission.

Mobilizing the Army for God's Great Commission

━━ David Platt ━━

It was while the church at Antioch was worshipping and fasting and praying that the Holy Spirit said, "Set apart for me Barnabas and Saul for the work to which I have called them" (Acts 13:2). I've often wondered how that happened. Exactly how did the Holy Spirit *say* that?

I don't know the answer to that question, but I do know that as a result of what the Holy Spirit *said* on that day, a missionary movement was born that led to the spread of the gospel throughout the known world in the first century. The contributors to this book have had a goal in these chapters: that God, in his grace and by his Spirit, might see fit to set apart men and women for the spread of his gospel to those who have never heard it. To that end, I want to urge you to consider what your role is in cross-cultural missions and to commit to follow the Lord of the Harvest however he leads. For those who are prepared to make this commitment, let me clarify what such a commitment means.

A Call to Commitment and a Clarification

I am not calling people to move tomorrow to the Middle East. I am not calling people to make a rash vow based upon manipulated emotion. And I am not calling people to make this decision alone—that's why I want to emphasize that what you might resolve to do is to go to your church and say, "I want to be sent. I want to be sent as a missionary, as one who crosses a culture to spend my life for the spread of the gospel." That's the moment toward which of all of this is headed.

I want to call every follower of Christ to put a blank check on the table with your life before God, and to say, "Whatever you want me to do, I will do it. Wherever you want me to go, I will go. No strings attached." Ask God with open hands, "Are you leading me to go? Are you redirecting my future (even my family's future) toward life among the nations?"

I'm Moving On

Over and over again in this book, we have referenced Paul's epistle to the Romans. In particular, we have highlighted Romans 15:18–21, when Paul summarizes his ministry and says,

I will not venture to speak of anything except what Christ has accomplished through me to bring the Gentiles to obedience— by word and deed, by the power of signs and wonders, by the power of the Spirit of God—so that from Jerusalem and all the way around to Illyricum I have fulfilled the ministry of the gospel of Christ; and thus I make it my ambition to preach the gospel, not where Christ has already been named, lest I build on someone else's foundation, but as it is written, "Those who have never been told of him will see, and those who have never heard will understand."

Here Paul expresses his calling to be a missionary—to spend his life crossing cultures for the spread of the gospel among unreached people. In Romans 15, he says, "I want to go to regions where the gospel is not." And because he has fully proclaimed the gospel from Jerusalem all the way around to Illyricum (nearly 1,500 miles away), he says in verse 23, "I no longer have any room for work in these regions."

That's a strange thing to say. Paul looks around him at Corinth and Ephesus and Crete and says, "There's no more work for me to do here—I'm moving on."

Did that mean that everyone in those cities had been saved? Did that even mean that everybody in those cities had heard the gospel? No. What it meant was that the church had been planted in those cities. The gospel had been proclaimed, disciples had been made, the church had been founded, and work was going on. So Paul says, "I'm moving on."

No Second-Class Citizens

We know from the rest of the New Testament that there were other people that Paul himself told to stay in those places. Paul told Timothy to stay and pastor the church in Ephesus (1 Tim. 1:3). He told Titus to stay in Crete (Titus 1:5). So the picture we see in the New Testament is of some Christians *staying* under the sovereignty of God in certain places that have already been reached with the gospel (remember, there were other leaders at the church at Antioch that the Holy Spirit *didn't* set apart to go), and then we see other Christians, like Paul and some of his companions, who are moving to other cities and regions to plant new churches. And it's not because Paul is being obedient and everyone else is being disobedient, but rather because God is calling his people to carry out this mission in different places among different peoples.

Here I want to be especially careful. In no way do I want to imply that those who don't move to live as a missionary among unreached peoples are second-class citizens in the kingdom of God. The ultimate issue is not whether you stay or go; the ultimate issue is whether you obey. For some, obedience will mean staying. For others, obedience will mean going. But for everyone, obedience will mean setting the trajectory of our lives, regardless of where we live, toward praying and giving and working and longing and laboring for the spread of the gospel to those who've never heard—whether we do that from Birmingham, Alabama, or Bihar, India, or anywhere in between. That's the whole reason why Paul writes the letter to the Romans in the first place. Consider what he says in the verses that follow:

This is the reason why I have so often been hindered from coming to you. But now, since I no longer have any room for work in these regions, and since I have longed for many years to come to you, I hope to see you in passing as I go to Spain, and to be helped on my journey there by you, once I have enjoyed your company for a while. At present, however, I am going to Jerusalem bringing aid to the saints. (Rom. 15:22–25)

Some historical background around Paul's missionary journeys will hopefully help you understand what's going on here in Romans:

- *Paul's First Missionary Journey:* On Paul's first missionary journey, he was sent out by Antioch, which is where the Lord said, "Set apart for me Barnabas and Saul for the work to which I have called them" (Acts 13:2). Then, after this journey, Barnabas and Saul came back to Antioch where they encouraged the saints again.
- *Paul's Second Missionary Journey:* The church at Antioch sent Paul out again on a second missionary journey, during which he went north to some of the same places he had gone

before. It's at this time that he received the Macedonian call, a vision with a man of Macedonia saying, "Come over to Macedonia and help us" (Acts 16:9). So Paul went north into Macedonia into places like Thessalonica and Corinth, and then he came down to Ephesus and he made his way to Jerusalem. Then he went back to Antioch, his home base, and he encouraged the saints there at the end of his second missionary journey.

- *Paul's Third Missionary Journey:* On the third missionary journey, Paul went out again from Antioch and he retraced his steps and encouraged the churches where he had already preached. During this third missionary journey, Paul arrived in Corinth and wrote this letter to the church at Rome. He told them he was traveling to Jerusalem, yet he did not mention any plans of going back to Antioch. But why not? Because ultimately he wanted to go to Spain, and going back to Antioch was not the best way to get to Spain. So Paul wrote this letter from Corinth to Rome with Spain in his view. And he says to the church at Rome, "I want you to help me get the gospel to Spain."

Paul's letter to the Romans, then, is somewhat like a missionary support letter. He is writing to encourage the believers at Rome to take the gospel to the nations, and he wants the whole church involved. He's not writing to the church at Rome, saying, "All of you are called to be missionaries with me, and the entire church at Rome needs to go with me to Spain." No, he's writing to say, "I need you to help me on my journey there, to send me out, and maybe some of you should be *sent* with me, but regardless all of you should *join* with me in an effort to get the gospel to Spain." Paul wants them to pray with him, just like he urges them to do in verse 30 regarding his trip to Jerusalem—to strive together with him in prayers to God. Paul also wants them to give to him. The clear implication of verse

24 is that Paul is hoping they will help him financially in getting the gospel to Spain.

Shifting Our Missions-Funding Paradigm

As a side note (but I believe an important one), it is important to realize that missions in the New Testament was funded in a variety of ways. Even with Paul, this is true. Sometimes he was fully providing for himself; other times he was leaning on help from other churches. I believe this must be a huge factor as we consider *going* on mission. When many people think of a missionary, they think of a fully financially supported gospel worker, which is good. This is how many missionaries are serving around the world and will serve around the world in the days to come—giving themselves full-time to making disciples and multiplying churches, all while raising or receiving full financial support from senders. But there are other pictures of missionaries that are possible, including partially supported or even self-supported missionaries who have some sort of income stream wherever they're serving as a missionary. If we want to blow the lid off the number of missionaries in the world, we must expand our paradigm here.

Think about how we see the gospel spreading throughout the book of Acts. In Acts 8, after Stephen was stoned, the Bible tells us that everyone in the church, except the apostles, scattered from Jerusalem, proclaiming the gospel wherever they went (Acts 8:1–4). And do you know who started the church at Antioch that sent out these missionaries? It wasn't Paul, and it wasn't any other apostle. It was unnamed, ordinary Christians who were scattered after the persecution of Stephen.

This is the same story we see in the pages that follow in Acts, as men and women hear the gospel from Paul in places like Ephesus as they're traveling through on business. Then they take the gospel from Ephesus throughout all of Asia. Paul's ministry in Ephesus is described this way: "This continued for two years, so that all the residents of Asia heard the word of the Lord, both Jews and Greeks" (Acts 19:10). So you have workers with different vocations who are going into different locations. Without question, this is a significant way that the gospel is going to spread to more than six thousand unreached people groups today.

You don't get into unreached people groups with a missionary visa. You don't go to Saudi Arabia and say, "I'm called to be a missionary and convert Muslims to Christianity." Missionaries, in that sense, can't get into Saudi Arabia. But do you know who can? Followers of Christ in all sorts of business fields, who can travel periodically to Saudi Arabia, who can move there and work there, and in the process, bring the gospel there. Do you realize there are about six million Americans living abroad right now, and estimates are that over one million of those are evangelical Christians? Do we realize what a missions force this can be in the world? Oh, this is why, even when we talk about missions, you don't need to just think, "Okay, I need to quit school, leave my job, and throw it all away to reach the nations." No, instead we must each ask, "Is there a way that my education, my job, or my skills can be used to make the gospel known in one of the neediest places in the world?"

If we really want to reach all the peoples of the world with the gospel, it's going to happen in large part on the wings of workers—men and women with jobs—who stop assuming that they should teach or program computers or manage or do accounting or do sales or practice medicine among the reached. It's going to happen when workers default to the fact that if there are this many people groups around the world who have never even heard the gospel, then maybe God has given us an education, job, and skills to reach them.

What if God has designed the globalization of today's marketplace for the spread of his gospel through the sending of his people as workers around the world for the glory of his name?

Many Gifts—One Goal

So, coming back to Romans, Paul is writing to the church—the whole church—saying, "Let's work together to get the gospel to Spain." And he starts listing their names, all sorts of them. In Romans 16:3–15, Paul writes,

> Greet Prisca and Aquila, my fellow workers in Christ Jesus, who risked their necks for my life, to whom not only I give thanks but all the churches of the Gentiles give thanks as well. Greet also the church in their house. Greet my beloved Epaenetus, who was the first convert to Christ in Asia. Greet Mary, who has worked hard for you. Greet Andronicus and Junia, my kinsmen and my fellow prisoners. They are well known to the apostles, and they were in Christ before me. Greet Ampliatus, my beloved in the Lord. Greet Urbanus, our fellow worker in Christ, and my beloved Stachys. Greet Apelles, who is approved in Christ. Greet those who belong to the family of Aristobulus. Greet my kinsman Herodion. Greet those in the Lord who belong to the family of Narcissus. Greet those workers in the Lord, Tryphaena and Tryphosa. Greet the beloved Persis, who has worked hard in the Lord. Greet Rufus, chosen in the Lord; also his mother, who has been a mother to me as well. Greet Asyncritus, Phlegon, Hermes, Patrobas, Hermas, and the brothers who are with them. Greet Philologus, Julia, Nereus and his sister, and Olympas, and all the saints who are with them.

We have this list of twenty-six different people who are play-ing different roles and doing different things in the mission of the church. We see Prisca and Aquila, a couple who served with Paul in Ephesus and now lived in Rome. We see Epaenetus, the first to come to Christ in Asia, and then another couple, Andronicus and Junia, who were in prison for Christ alongside Paul. We see men and women, families and households, single and married, young and old, rich and poor. We see Rufus and his mom, who was like a mother to Paul. All kinds of different people *brought together* by the *person* of Christ and *united together* on the *mission* of Christ. And Paul is saying to them all, "Together, we need to get the gospel to Spain." That is going to involve us doing different things—praying, giving, going, and working to get the gospel to those who've never heard.

That is the picture I have in my mind when I think about mobi-lizing the church for missions today—different people with unique gifts, unique passions, unique skills, and unique opportunities alto-gether saying, "Let's take the gospel to unreached people." With more than six thousand unreached people groups, this mission is going to involve many of us going to make disciples of Christ as missionaries in another culture. It is going to involve others of us making disciples right where we live now and praying, giving, supporting, and stand-ing with those whom God calls to go. In the end, it is going to involve an army of God's people mobilized for the Great Commission.

So, the question I've been asking is, "How do you mobilize God's people to give their lives to this Great Commission?" How do you mobilize people to go totally against the grain of the culture around them—even in many ways against the grain of the church culture around them—to willingly lay down their lives, to gladly put aside their possessions, and to sacrificially spend themselves for the sake of unreached peoples? How do you bring people to have that kind of resolve?

The Word of God as the Fuel for Missions

This is where Romans is so instructive. Paul wants to get the gospel to Spain, where they've never heard, but notice what he doesn't do. Paul doesn't write a letter in which he tells them about all the needs in Spain and about various stories of these people or that village. Instead, he writes a letter in which he gives them quite possibly the most logical and systematically reasoned presentation of the gospel that we have in all of the Bible.

Maybe Mack Stiles is right, and the missionary call, first and foremost, is informed by God's Word and inspired by his gospel. And maybe, just maybe, if Jesus might bring us to a deeper reverence for this Word, and a deeper love for this gospel, then the inevitable result would be a death-defying resolve to go to unreached peoples, no matter how difficult or dangerous that might be.

You see, there was a day when the people of God greatly revered the Word of God. They would gather together in scenes like we see in Nehemiah 8, and all it would take was the opening of the Scriptures and immediately everyone would stand to their feet (Neh. 8:5). Not only would they stand, but as the Book was read, they would also raise their hands in worship. They would cry aloud, "Amen! Amen!" The people would bow down in worship with their faces to the ground. It was all-out worship in response to the written Word of God.

Now, twenty-five hundred years later, it seems things have changed. What do we equate those sorts of actions with in our worship—people standing, raising their hands, calling out, and maybe if they're extreme, bowing down with their faces on the ground? We do these things when the music starts. All it takes in our day is the strum of a guitar, and we are on our feet, and we are lifting our hands, and we are shouting out. Is this a bad thing? Absolutely not. Nehemiah 12:27–47 is a glorious picture of musical worship. But the question I want to ask is, What if we were a people, a generation, who responded to God's Word like that? What if all it took was the proclamation of the pure and powerful Word of God to bring us to our feet, to send our arms and hands into the air, to cause us to cry out, "Amen! Amen!" and even to bow down unashamedly in the assembly with our faces to the ground, not thinking about what people might perceive, but provoked to lie prostrate before the God of this Book?

What if all it took was the Scriptures to inspire that kind of worship? What if God's Word had that kind of authority among us and roused that kind of affection in us? What if we loved God's words like that? What if we revered them and honored them and submitted our lives to them like that?

And what if we were truly inspired by God's gospel—this good news that the just and gracious God of the universe looked upon hopelessly sinful people and sent his Son, Jesus Christ, God in the flesh, to bear his wrath against sin on the cross and to show his power over sin in the resurrection so that all who have faith in him will be reconciled to God forever? Romans even says that hypothetically this gospel is good enough to throw yourself into hell so that other people can have it. After eight chapters of rich gospel exposition, here is what Paul says in Romans 9:1–5:

> I am speaking the truth in Christ—I am not lying; my con-science bears me witness in the Holy Spirit—that I have great sorrow and unceasing anguish in my heart. For I could wish that I myself were accursed and cut off from Christ for the sake of my brothers, my kinsmen according to the flesh. They are Israelites, and to them belong the adoption, the glory, the cov-enants, the giving of the law, the worship, and the promises. To them belong the patriarchs, and from their race, according to the flesh, is the Christ, who is God over all, blessed forever. Amen.

I don't know if there is a passage anywhere else in Scripture that more clearly links *the beauty of the gospel with the burden of mission.* Paul says with great sorrow and unceasing anguish, "Before God, I would go to hell if I could . . . I would throw myself into damnation . . . if that would mean the salvation of these people." I don't know how to comprehend that statement. To stand on the brink of everlasting darkness, eternal fire that will never end, and to say, "I would jump in—I would jump in right now—if that meant the Jewish people's salvation." These were Jewish people, mind you, who were persecuting Paul and waiting for him in Jerusalem to arrest him and have him killed. And Paul says to them, "I'd go to hell forever for you." How do you say that?

Now it's different in significant ways, but think for a moment about an unreached people group today. Think about an unreached people group that is producing terrorists who are intent on killing you. Think about an unreached people group that is waiting to arrest or murder you and your family when you come their way. How do you say, "I would throw myself into hell forever if that meant you might be saved. But, since I can't, I'll do whatever it takes for your salvation. I'll lay down my life, my family, and my future, so that you might be saved"—how do you say that and mean it?

Saved by This Gospel

Here's how. Whether you are going to live among unreached people groups or not, remember three things when you face obstacles, challenges, and loss, and when you don't know if you can go on, particularly for the sake of people who oppose you at every level.

First, in those moments, *remember how you've been saved by this gospel.* Remember that you yourself were once under the wrath of God, deserving of eternal damnation—that hell is your rightful destination. Remember that God, the very God whom you rebelled against, came running after you to redeem you. And how did he do that? He did that by embracing the judgment you deserve. He redeemed us by putting himself in our place on a cross, where he bore God's wrath in our stead. Then, though we had absolutely nothing to do with where we were born, he put you and me in a place and he guided us on a path where we have heard the gospel. Though our eyes were blind to its beauty, his grace broke through our hard hearts, and he opened our eyes to believe. He saved us, not because of any merit in us, but solely because of mercy in him. He predestined, called, and justified us, and he has promised to glorify us with him forever (Rom. 8:29–30).

So now it just makes sense, as sinners saved by this gospel, to go to the most rebellious, the hardest-to-reach, the most resistant people, and to lay down our lives in love for the sake of their salvation. We owe it to them. That's what Paul says: "I am under obligation both to Greeks and to barbarians, both to the wise and to the foolish" (Rom. 1:14). I'm *obligated*! Paul says, "I owe the nations the gospel." We owe the gospel to the world. Let that soak in. *Saved people this side of heaven owe the gospel to lost peoples this side of hell.*

Sent by This God

Second, as you reach out to the unreached, *realize that you've been sent by this God*. Paul is a servant, a slave, of Christ. He is "set apart for the gospel of God" (Rom. 1:1) and sent out with the gospel by God. In Romans 10:15, Paul says we preach the gospel because we've been sent by God. Think of it: *God* is sending *you*! This is a breathtaking thought. In all this talk about *senders*, don't forget who the real Sender is—with a capital "S." And why has he sent us? There are three reasons, but they each make essentially the same point. You can't disconnect one from another.

First, God has sent us *for their salvation*. When we're talking about unreached peoples, we're talking about individuals (boys and girls, men and women) who are born and live and die and never even hear the gospel of Jesus Christ. But understand this: they do hear about God. More precisely, they "see" God. That's what Romans 1:19 says: God makes himself "plain to them." Every unreached person in the world has some knowledge of God. Whether it's a man in the African desert, a woman in an Asian village, or a tribe in the Amazon rainforest—even if they haven't heard the gospel of Christ, they've seen the glory of God in the world he has made. But they've also rejected him, just like we all have in our sin. Romans 1:21 says, "Although they knew God, they did not honor him as God or give thanks to him, but they became futile in their thinking, and their foolish hearts were darkened."

College students ask me all the time, "What about the innocent guy in Africa who's never heard the gospel—what happens to him when he dies?" I say, "He goes to heaven, without question." The only problem is, he doesn't exist! There is no innocent guy in Africa. If there was, he wouldn't need the gospel, because he's innocent. He'd go to heaven because he has no sin. The problem is: there are no innocent unreached people in the world. Every unreached person in the world is guilty before God. That's why they need the gospel.

Once we put these truths together, we must realize what this means: *there are over two billion people in the world today whose knowledge of God is only sufficient to damn them to hell forever.* They have knowledge that God exists, and without exception they have rejected him. They deserve his wrath, and that's the end of the story for them. They have never heard the name of Jesus, the One who can save them from their sins. The God who sends us is the God who has revealed himself in the majesty of mountains and hills and rivers and oceans and the mysteries of the universe. This God has sent you and me with an even greater revelation of himself—the revelation that this God has made a way for our salvation!

Second, God sends us *for his exaltation.* This is more than mere altruism for Paul in Romans 9. Why is Paul so anguished in those verses? Listen to the way he talks about the Jewish people: "They are Israelites, and to them belong the adoption, the glory, the covenants, the giving of the law, the worship, and the promises. To them belong the patriarchs, and from their race, according to the flesh, is the Christ, who is God over all!" (Rom. 9:4–5). This is the people of God, Paul says, the people that God bound his name and his glory and his honor to going all the way back to Genesis 12. The glory of God is at stake in this people, which is why, immediately after this in verse 6, he says, "But it is not as though the word of God has failed."

In the rest of Romans 9, 10, and 11, Paul is zealous to show that God *is* sovereign over the salvation of his people and God *will* be faithful to his promises. Although it's in a different context, Revelation 5 also tells us about a promise God will keep, for Jesus has purchased men and women from every people, tribe, tongue, and nation (Rev. 5:9). But when you look at the world with six thousand unreached people groups, it's tempting to think, *Is God really going to save people from all of them? Is God really sovereign over salvation? Is God really going to be faithful to his promise?*

The Bible is beckoning us to great sorrow and unceasing anguish because we have brothers and sisters whom God has promised to adopt as sons and daughters, and our Father is sending us to bring them into the family that they might know the joy and the love and the hope and the wonder and the grace and the mercy and the grandeur and the glory of our God. There are around sixteen thousand people groups in the world, and six thousand of them are unreached. So why do we have great sorrow and unceasing anguish? *Because our God is worthy to receive praise from 6,000 more people groups on the planet.*

Finally, God not only sends us for the salvation of unreached people groups and for his exaltation, but, also *for our satisfaction*. That is, for our good. I know that putting a blank check on the table with your life and your family and your future is a scary proposition for many of us. After all, what if God says to go to Afghanistan to work among the Taliban—is that what I'm going to do with my life? What about a husband or a wife? What about kids? I could lose everything. The thought of a blank check with your life may be frightening to you, but don't forget *who* you're giving the blank check to. If you can trust God to redeem you, then you can trust God to lead you. If you can trust God to save you for eternity, you can trust God to satisfy you on earth. What we really need to be afraid of are any conditions we might put upon our obedience to God.

Consider this: the God who is sending you to difficult, dangerous places to reach peoples is the God who is sovereign over every single one of those peoples and places. Do you realize what that means? That means nothing can happen to you on the field as a missionary that is outside of the gracious hands of a sovereign God. That doesn't mean suffering won't come, and it doesn't mean death won't come. But remember this truth in that moment *ten* years from now when you're on the field and everything is falling apart: nothing is happening or can happen to you outside of the sovereign will of a good and gracious God who has promised to satisfy you for the next ten *trillion* years.

Secure in This Great Commission

All this leads to the last reason we can say, "I'll do whatever it takes and give whatever it costs—I'd throw myself into hell if I could for the sake of a people group's salvation." That reason is because we can *rest completely secure in this Great Commission*. It is going to happen. Disciples are going to be made in every nation. Jesus said in Matthew 24:14, "This gospel of the kingdom will be proclaimed throughout the whole world as a testimony to all nations, and then the end will come."

People ask, "Do you really believe when all the nations have been reached with the gospel, the end is going to come?" My response is, "Well, Jesus said it." Then people say, "Well, how do you know our definition of people groups is right? Or how do you know when they are officially reached? And are you saying that Jesus couldn't come back today, because there are six thousand people groups still unreached?"

No, that's not what I'm saying. Jesus could come back today. We don't know for sure exactly what is meant by "people groups" or the idea of being "reached"—these are our best estimates when it comes to the *ethne*, or "peoples," of the world. But I can't improve at this point on the words of George Ladd, who called Matthew 24:14 "the single most important verse in the Word of God for the people of God today." Ladd says,

> God alone knows the definition of terms. I cannot precisely define who all the nations are, but I do not need to know. I know only one thing: Christ has not yet returned; therefore, the task is not yet done. When it is done, Christ will come. Our responsibility is not to insist on defining the terms; our responsibility is to complete the task. So long as Christ does not return, our work is undone. Let us get busy and complete our mission.[30]

Even if you debate exactly how Matthew 24:14 should be interpreted, then jump to the back of the Book where Jesus, in the end, is surrounded by a great multitude that no one can count from every nation, from all tribes and peoples and languages, who are standing before him clothed in white robes crying out with a loud voice, "Salvation belongs to our God who sits on the throne, and to the Lamb!" (Rev. 7:10). Only a few verses later John says of these individuals,

> Therefore they are before the throne of God,
>   and serve him day and night in his temple;
>   and he who sits on the throne will shelter them with his
>   presence.
> They shall hunger no more, neither thirst anymore;
>   the sun shall not strike them,
>   nor any scorching heat,
> For the Lamb in the midst of the throne will be their shepherd,
>   and he will guide them to springs of living water,
> and God will wipe away every tear from their eyes.
>   (Rev. 7:15–17)

We give our lives in anticipation of that day.

So Who Will Go?

Paul gave his life in anticipation of that last day, and the Lord of the Harvest used it in great ways for the spread of his gospel. Of course, Paul wasn't the only one sharing the gospel, but it's safe to say that he made a significant impact in his day. Yet, as far as we know, the gospel had not penetrated Spain by the time Paul died. Did that mean Paul failed? Was he not able to accomplish what God had told him to do—to get the gospel to Spain?

Before we come to that conclusion, we need to consider the situation in Spain within a mere two hundred years after Paul's death. In that short time frame, Spain had many known Christians throughout the country, and the church had spread throughout the surrounding regions. Never underestimate what happens not only in our lives but beyond our lives when the church is sending and Christians are going to those who need the gospel.

In light of the way Jesus used Paul and those early Christians, and in light of the concentrations of unreached people groups in the world today, I want to ask the question—inspired by God's Word, and informed by his gospel—is Jesus setting you apart to go?

God Is Finishing His Mission Now

What Happened at the First Cross Conference

John Piper

For many of us, it was a dream come true when about thirty-six thousand college students met in Louisville, Kentucky, December 27–30, 2013, to consider the global glory of Christ, the nature of Christ's mission to the unreached peoples of the world, and the power of the Christian gospel.

Here was a conference on missions for students with a resounding focus on

- the sovereignty of God's grace in the salvation of sinners (Acts 13:48),
- the wrath of God over all mankind as the greatest threat to the world (John 3:36),
- the terrible reality of eternal suffering (Matt. 25:46),

- the greatness of God's mercy in propitiating his own wrath in Christ (Rom. 3:25–26),
- the necessity of hearing the gospel of Christ in order to be saved (Rom. 10:13–17),
- the stupendous Reformation truth of justification by faith alone (Rom. 4:4–5),
- the compassion of missionaries who are called to suffer for the good of all men, especially the eternal good (Gal. 6:10),
- the necessity of reaching all the peoples of the earth and the motivating certainty that God has a people in each one (Rev. 5:9; Acts 18:10),
- and the summons to joyfully sacrifice anything to reach these nations, because to die is gain (Phil. 1:21).

In other words, this conference—which we called Cross—was the fruit and overflow of an awakening in our day to the glory of God's sovereign grace.

- Call it Reformed theology.
- Call it the doctrines of grace.
- Call it the new Calvinism.
- Call it Big God theology.
- Call it a passion for God's supremacy in all things.
- Call it the resurgence of God-centered, Christ-exalting, Bible-saturated worship.
- Call it a vision of a great, holy, just, wise, good, gracious, sovereign God whose throne is established in the heavens and who does whatever he pleases.
- Call it what you will.

God is doing this—God is awakening millions of people all over the world, especially young people, to these stunning and glorious realities. This conference was a fruit of this awakening.

Something Much Bigger

It is also part of something much bigger than this theological awakening. For the last forty years, amazing things have been happening in the world to advance the spread of the salvation of Christ among the unreached peoples of the world. For example,

The 1990s saw the most concerted attempt to analyze the need of the world. . . . 1995 saw the beginning of the Joshua Project List (JPL), originally a list of 1,583 of the world's least reached peoples. While this is expanded to now include all the peoples in the world (16,583), the original list served as a catalyst for the Church to pray for, adopt, and engage with every one of these least reached peoples. It also inspired national-level research in many countries where the 1,583 were found; this missiological and people group research by Majority World Christians has been a major step toward the completion of the Great Commission.[31]

The generation just past was one of the most remarkable in the history of missions. Things thought impossible have become reality. For example,

Patrick Johnstone, when queried in 1979 about the most difficult places for gospel breakthrough, named Mongolia and Albania. Today, there are at least 40,000 Mongolian believers. Albania is open and churches are growing. Who among us, 30 years ago, could have envisioned over 100 million Chinese Christians, massive people movements in Iran, Algeria, and Sudan, breakthroughs in Mozambique, Cambodia, and Nepal, and the beginnings of freedom for hundreds of millions of oppressed in India? Only God![32]

This recent history is unprecedented not only because of break-throughs in who has been reached, but also because of who is being sent. Missions is not from the West alone, but from everywhere to everywhere. There has been an explosion of sending countries and sending agencies. Consider these remarkable facts:

- "Today, there are over 4,000 known evangelical mission agencies sending out 250,000 missionaries from over 200 countries. This is up from 1,800 known mission agencies and 70,000 missionaries in 1980."[33]

- "And nearly half of the world's top missionary-sending countries are now located in the global South."

- "Of the ten countries sending the most missionaries in 2010, three were in the global South: Brazil, South Korea, and India."

- "Other notable missionary senders included South Africa, the Philippines, Mexico, China, Colombia, and Nigeria."

- "The United States still tops the chart by far in terms of total missionaries, sending 127,000 in 2010 compared to the 34,000 sent by No. 2-ranked Brazil."

- Looked at another way, not in raw numbers, but missionaries sent per million church members—Palestine comes out on top at 3,401 sent, followed by Ireland, Malta, and Samoa.

- "South Korea ranks No. 5 at 1,014 missionaries sent per million church members, a sign of the continued strength of its missions movement compared to the No. 9-ranked United States at 614 missionaries sent."

- "The country that received the most missionaries in 2010? The United States, with 32,400 sent from other nations."[34]

This is a fraction of the bigger picture that the Cross conference is a part of. We have no illusions of grandeur. God's world is massive. And God is infinitely more massive in power and wisdom and goodness. He will finish his mission.[35] The peoples of the world will be reached. And he will use people of many different Christian persuasions to do it, not just Calvinists.

Glory Gone Global

God is passionate for his glory among the nations. He raised Jesus from the dead and exalted him over all "so that at the name of Jesus every knee should bow . . . to the glory of God the Father" (Phil. 2:9–11). In other words, *God* exalted Jesus for the glory of *God*. Nothing will stop him from having a people who love to ascribe all glory to him in the great work of salvation.

Some theologies are driven more fully by this vision than others. The Cross conference is a dream come true because this is the engine that drives everything—the glory of God's sovereign grace in salvation—accomplished, applied, heralded—globally.

APPENDIX 2

What Is Cross?

Cross exists for the global purpose of magnifying the kingly majesty of Jesus Christ. Our focus is on all the unreached peoples of the world where Jesus is not worshiped as God and Savior.

To that end, Cross aims to mobilize students for the most dangerous and loving cause in the universe: rescuing people from eternal suffering and bringing them into the everlasting joy of friendship with Jesus.

Jesus said that every person without faith in him remains under the wrath of God (John 3:36). He also said that God did not send him "to condemn the world, but in order that the world might be saved through him" (John 3:17).

That saving faith is born through the message of Jesus' blood and righteousness—his cross. Everyone who believes is saved. But nobody believes without a messenger.

World missions is the glorious gospel enterprise of going like Christ into another cultural world to rescue people from eternal suffering, and renovate their broken lives, that they might render to God the splendor of his majesty through faith in Christ.

There is no better reason to lose your life and no greater way to live it.

Our Story

Over the past few years, several pastors and church leaders, quite independently from each other, began to feel a burden for a new student missions conference that would trumpet the global majesty of God's sovereign grace, the gospel passion of Christ to rescue people from eternal suffering, and the remaining task of planting the church among the unreached and unengaged peoples of the world.

The Cross Leadership Team is the result of this burden and vision. From different backgrounds and with different ministry experiences we have come together for this purpose. We are not a church. We are not a new campus ministry. We are not an offshoot of any existing ministry, as thankful as we are for so many likeminded movements and organizations. Our aim is simpler and more focused: We want to host a conference that, we pray, may be used of God to mobilize students in the cause of frontier missions for the global glory of Jesus Christ. That's our passion, our purpose.

Cross is a student missions conference . . .

- for worshipping the Lord Jesus Christ,
  - » who upholds the universe by the word of his power,
  - » has absolute authority over all the nations and peoples of earth,
  - » freely offers to all forgiveness of sins on the basis of his death and resurrection,
  - » summons all the peoples of earth to repent and believe in his name,
  - » and gives eternal joy in his presence to all who do.
- for centering on the gospel of God concerning the death and resurrection of his Son—the only message by which God saves from his own wrath those who hear and believe.

- for clarifying Christ's saving mission to the unreached peoples of the world, providing solid, biblical foundations for that mission in doctrines of sovereign grace.
- for praying to the Lord of the harvest that he might send out laborers into his harvest.
- for emboldening thousands with biblical truth to embrace the mission and go to the peoples yet unreached.
- for sobering all with the prospect of inevitable suffering for the sake of Christ's name.
- for connecting goers with persons and churches and agencies who will help equip and position them for maximum gospel-spreading among the unreached peoples for the name of Christ.

And thus for . . .

- obeying the command of the Lord to make disciples of all nations,
- pressing with eagerness toward the coming of Christ,
- preparing for the Lord Jesus the reward of his suffering,
- relieving as much suffering as we can, especially eternal suffering,
- loving our neighbor by giving our lives for the greatest and longest good of the world,
- and fulfilling the purpose for which God created the world— that the earth would be full of the glory of the Lord as the waters cover the sea.

The Cross Leadership Team
Thabiti Anyabwile   *Zane Pratt*
Kevin DeYoung   *David Sitton*
John Piper   *Mack Stiles*
David Platt

Note: The Cross Affirmation of Faith is available online at http://crosscon.com/2013/03/cross-affirmation-of-faith

Why a New Student Missions Conference?

━━━━━━ John Piper ━━━━━━

As a member of the Cross Leadership Team that conceived and launched the Cross conference, I am thrilled to be part of it. Here is my seven-point answer to why this conference exists.

1. With seven thousand schools of higher learning, and fifteen million students, and a spread of five thousand miles (from Maine to Hawaii), there is room in America for another conference about the most important issue in the world.

2. In fact, we believe that God is stirring among young people today not unlike he was in the Student Volunteer Movement a hundred years ago. Between 1886 and 1910, this movement sent out 4,338 missionaries. Over 50 percent of all missionaries from America between 1906 and 1909 were Student Volunteers. We would like to join others in helping students lift their sails into this new wind of the Spirit.

3. More specifically, we see a growing tide of students with a big view of God as sovereign and glorious. This tide has been fed by decades of God-exalting worship music, Bible-saturated campus

ministries, and the book-publishing and social-media explosion of the Reformed resurgence. In other words, there are thousands of students eager to plug the cord of their passion into the great biblical truths of the Reformation. They care about building their lives and ministries on robust theology. We want to point that tide to the unreached peoples of the world.

4. We are driven by what John Stott called a passion "for His Imperial Majesty, Jesus Christ, and for the glory of his empire." For all we know, America may be a footnote in history someday, and every President virtually forgotten, like the Caesars of Rome. But we know beyond all doubt that the kingdom of Christ "shall never be destroyed. . . . It shall break in pieces all these kingdoms and bring them to an end, and it shall stand forever" (Dan. 2:44).

Christ's kingdom will triumph without sword or gun or bomb, because Jesus said, "My kingdom is not of this world. If my kingdom were of this world, my servants would have been fighting" (John 18:36). Bold and brokenhearted emissaries of Christ will conquer, not with weapons of the flesh, but "by the blood of the Lamb and by the word of their testimony, for they loved not their lives even unto death" (Rev. 12:11). We want to call students to this path of sacrificial triumph.

5. We are awakened to the terrible reality of eternal suffering, the universal scope of human fallenness, and the absolute necessity of hearing and believing the gospel of Jesus in order to be saved (Rom. 10:13–17).[36] One of the flags we want to wave over every generation of students is: "Followers of Jesus care about all suffering, especially eternal suffering."

Jesus spared the leper, and Jesus spoke of hell. Nobody in the Bible spoke so much of eternal suffering as Jesus did. We believe all humans are headed there unless they hear and believe the gospel of Jesus. God has put the remedy in our hands. The gospel is the power of God unto salvation. We have the joyful news that God sent his

Son into the world not to judge the world but that the world through him might be saved (John 3:17). We want to mobilize thousands of students under this flag.

6. We see the unique task of the missionary to be taking the gospel to the unreached and unengaged peoples of the world. God calls many Christians to many other worthy ministries. But missions is the glorious calling to learn a language, cross a culture, and speak the gospel in order to plant the church of Jesus among a people group with no cultural access to the gospel.

There are about 3,100 people groups in the world that are "unengaged"—that is, there is no known plan being implemented to reach them with the biblical gospel. We want that fact to be prominent in our conference. Under Christ and his gospel, that is our focus.

7. We believe that this kind of focus and this kind of student are an explosive combination. That is why Cross exists. We would like to bring them together and see what the Holy Spirit might detonate.

NOTES

1. "Inescapably hedonistic" is John Piper's description of Jesus' argument in Mark 8:34–35 in *Desiring God: Meditations of a Christian Hedonist* (Colorado Springs: Multnomah, 2011), 241.

2. Typically the label "unreached" means less than two percent evangelical Christians, and less than five percent total Christians. The 1982 Lausanne committee meeting in Chicago defined "people group" as "the largest group within which the gospel can spread as a church planting movement without encountering barriers of understanding or acceptance."

3. These definitions are based on the criteria at joshuaproject.net, which is a reputable tracker of the world's total people groups (more than 16,000) and how many among them are unreached (almost 7,000). The International Mission Board (imb.org) counts more than 11,000 total peoples, more than 6,500 of them unreached, and 3,000 unengaged. As of late 2014, the IMB lists 343 unengaged peoples with a population of more than 100,000.

4. Piper, *Desiring God*, 232.

5. Patrick Johnstone, *The Church Is Bigger Than You Think* (Tain, Scotland: Christian Focus Pub., 1998), 105.

6. John Newton (1725–1807), pastor and writer of the hymn "Amazing Grace," observed the distinction between the missionary call and the call to labor among one's own reached people. He wrote in a letter to a fellow pastor, "A minister who should go to [an unreached people] without a call from the Lord, and without receiving from him an apostolical spirit, the spirit of a missionary, enabling him to forsake all, to give up all, to venture all, to put himself into the Lord's hands without reserve, to sink or swim, had better run his head against a stone wall. I am strongly inclined to hope Mr. Johnson is thus called, and will be thus qualified. I should not advise him to consult with you upon

this point. Your appointment is to smoke your pipe quietly at home, to preach, and to lecture to your pupils. You are not cut out for a missionary; and nothing, perhaps, would have been done either in the Danish West Indian Islands, or in Greenland, if the attachments and feelings of all men had been like yours and mine. I must have my tea, my regular hours, and twenty little things which I can have when my post is fixed. I should shrink at the thought of living upon seals and train oil." John Newton, *One Hundred and Twenty Nine Letters from the Rev. John Newton to the Rev. William Bull* (London: Hamilton, Adams, and Co., 1847), 219–20. Thanks to my coworker Tony Reinke for unearthing this quote from Newton.

7. D. A. Carson, *The Cross and Christian Ministry* (Grand Rapids, MI: Baker, 2004), 117.

8. Piper, *Desiring God*, 232–33.

9. Carson, *Cross and Christian Ministry*, 132. For more on the relationship between *mission* among the reached and *missions* to the unreached, see "The Seamless Garment of Christian Mission," available online at www.desiring-God.org/mission.

10. James M. Boice, *Romans, vol. 1, Justification by Grace: Romans 1–4* (Grand Rapids, MI: Baker, 2005), 129.

11. John Frame, *Salvation Belongs to the Lord* (Phillipsburg, NJ: P&R Publishing, 2006), 298.

12. John Murray, *The Epistle to the Romans* (Grand Rapids, MI: Eerdmans, 1955), 162–63; cited in Boice, *Romans*, 132.

13. Boice, *Romans*, 131.

14. J. I. Packer, *Knowing God* (Downers Grove, IL: InterVarsity Press, 1973), 134–35; cited in Boice, *Romans*, 131.

15. Credit is due to Jason Helopolous, my pastoral colleague, whose article on Calvinism and missions inspired and greatly informed this list: http://thegospel-coalition.org/blogs/kevindeyoung/2013/07/03/does-calvinism-kill-missions/.

16. C. S. Lewis, *Mere Christianity* (New York: Touchstone, 1996 [1943]), 178.

17. For more on this passage in Lewis, see Randy Alcorn's appendix in *The Romantic Rationalist: God, Life, and Imagination in the Work of C. S. Lewis,* edited by David Mathis and John Piper (Wheaton, IL: Crossway Books, 2014), 150–52.

18. John Newton, *Works of John Newton*, vol. 2 (London: 1824), 52.

19. As quoted by J. I. Packer in "Introductory Essay" to John Owen's *The Death of Death in the Death of Christ* (Edinburgh: Banner of Truth Trust, 1995), 14.

20. J. I. Packer "Introductory Essay" to John Owen's *The Death of Death in the Death of Christ* (Edinburgh: Banner of Truth Trust, 1995), 15.

21. For example, the Muslim Koran says, "That they said (in boast), 'We killed Christ Jesus the son of Mary, the Messenger of Allah'; but they killed him not, nor crucified him, but so it was made to appear to them, and those who differ therein are full of doubts, with no (certain) knowledge, but only conjecture to follow, for of a surety they killed him not." (See Surah 4:157, Yusuf Ali translation.)

22. For instance, the song "Jesus Was Way Cool" by King Missile.

23. See http://www.enterhisrest.org/testimonies/john_wesley.pdf.

24. Cicero, the Roman writer and statesman (106–43 BC), described crucifixion as the *summum supplicium,* the "ultimate punishment." See Cicero, *In Verrem* 2.5.168.

25. Quoted from Howard Guinness, *Sacrifice* (1936), in Lindsay Brown, *Shining Like Stars: The Power of the Gospel in the World's Universities* (Nottingham: InterVarsity Press, 2006), 151.

26. Michael Bennett, *Do You Feel Called by God?* (Sydney, Australia: Matthias Media, 2012).

27. Francis Schaeffer, *The Mark of a Christian* (Downers Grove, IL: InterVarsity Press, 1970).

28. See JoshuaProject.net.

29. Virginia Stem Owens, *The Reformed Journal* (Nov. 1983), 8.

30. George Eldon Ladd, *The Gospel of the Kingdom: Scriptural Studies in the Kingdom of God* (London: Paternoster, 1959), 137.

31. Jason Mandryk, *Operation World: The Definitive Prayer Guide to Every Nation* (Nottingham: InterVarsity Press, 2010).

32. Ibid., 4.

33. Global Network of Mission Structures, http://www.gnms.net/envisioning.html.

34. These bullet points are from a helpful article in *Christianity Today,* available online at http://www.christianitytoday.com/gleanings/2013/july/missionaries-countries-sent-received-csgc-gordon-conwell.html.

35. "Finish the mission" is the title of the recent book on global and local mission, edited by John Piper and David Mathis, with contributions from David Platt, Michael Oh, Louie Giglio, Ed Stetzer, and Michael Ramsden: *Finish the Mission: Bringing the Gospel to the Unreached and Unengaged* (Wheaton, IL: Crossway, 2012).

36. The Cross Affirmation of Faith is available online at http://crosscon.com/2013/03/cross-affirmation-of-faith.

SUBJECT AND PERSON INDEX

207

SCRIPTURE INDEX

desiringGod

Everyone wants to be happy. Our website was born and built for happiness. We want people everywhere to understand and embrace the truth that *God is most glorified in us when we are most satisfied in him.* We've collected more than thirty years of John Piper's speaking and writing, including translations into more than forty languages. We also provide a daily stream of new written, audio, and video resources to help you find truth, purpose, and satisfaction that never end. And it's all available free of charge, thanks to the generosity of people who've been blessed by the ministry.

If you want more resources for true happiness, or if you want to learn more about our work at Desiring God, we invite you to visit us at www.desiringGod.org.

www.desiringGod.org